ADVANCED ~~~~~~

"This is so much fun!! I always long for tomorrow when I will get to determine what exciting and fun things to do next. I am already dreading the day I have ticked off all the items from my to-do-list.

This guidance and approach has been a real eye-opener to me. I am the assistant of a CEO and aid our financial manager as well – and as such always have a thousand things going on at once! I thought I was really structured, but not compared to this – this is taking it to a whole new level.

So, thank you so much for writing this book, and I am happy to be one of those who has experienced a positive transformation in the way I work by following these steps."

Ingrid Wattman, Executive Assistant, BAE Systems Hägglunds

"This 31 day programme is time spent well, the recommended changes are manageable and easily adapted into daily practice. They really do help to bring structure into one's work and life habits."

Niklas Modig, Researcher, Speaker and Author of
This Is Lean, Stockholm School of Economics

"Well, it almost feels as if I have 'been saved' or something. I have read a whole bunch of similar books before but none of them have really given me what I need. Since I really wanted to give this a chance and I heard from my even more skeptical fiancé how well this had worked for him, I decided to become more structured. And I have – Hallelujah!"
Christina Tranebacke, CFO, Blue Art Promotion

"I'm on day 10 now in the structure book and I already notice the effect. I haven't been completely unstructured prior to reading it, but it has given food for thought and I have applied a few new tools and habits. I feel this great calm spread throughout my body; it is actually a physical sensation. Perhaps it is derived from the feeling of being in control, to know what needs to be done and what is still left to do. The uncompleted tasks don't spin around in my mind since I now have everything written down on the list and rest assured that I will not forget it."
Nina Lindman, Chief Information Officer,
Stormossen, Finland

"I have to say it feels just wonderful, I now go home every day feeling that I did what I needed to do."
Lillemor Sandh, Assistant, Mark Municipality

"Aided by your book, I now have tools that help me do the right thing at the right time, and feel CALM!! Absolutely wonderful. I feel that I am in charge of my life to a greater extent, as opposed to always having felt bossed around by others before."
Marie Larsson, Branch Manager, Mobility Services, Region Halland

"I feel more relaxed, safer and more focused since I now have so much more overview of all the things that need to get done."
Yvonne Crafoord, Payroll Manager, Stockholm Concert Hall

"I am usually very skeptical towards all kinds of quick-fixes and self-help solutions available for all kinds of problems. But after having spoken to my department manager and she had lent me your book, I have noticed a number of changes and improvements. It has now become easier and more fun to go to work every day."
Mats Genell, Project Manager, Karlstads Energi

"This is simply amazing, and I feel happy going to work every day now because I now finally have overview and a feeling of control."
Aini Stenseth Conn, Technical Consultant, Innovation Norway

"I now know what I need to do every day, I get things done faster and I never lay awake at night thinking about all the things I mustn't forget to do tomorrow or during the week."
Malin Nordgren, Sales Engineer, Gleitmo

"Even though I thought I was pretty structured before, I have now gotten to a whole new level of overviewing my tasks. It feels fantastic!"
Anna-Lena Hellgren, Sales & Marketing Assistant, Ivoclar Vivadent

"It feels very good to have gone through almost a third of the book and already notice how it has made a significant difference in my daily work, and it has even had positive 'spin-off effects' at home. I feel no need for 'rocket-science', but I do need something to lean against in order to take one small step at a time, and this is exactly what I get out of your book."
Jenny Skoglund, Recruitment Manager, Växjö Municipality

"I thought I was destined to do everything last minute… But from now on there will be no more waking up in the middle of the night and laying awake thinking about what I forgot to do!"
Ylva Prahl, Head of Operation, Karlskrona Municipality

"The feeling I have now after having completed ten days of the program is one of great relief and a slight sense of wonder. Relieved due to the control I feel I have gained. Wonder since I have gotten such a great overview of all my projects and previously scattered to-do-tasks in such a short time."
Johan Skyman, Specialty Gases Vendor, AGA Europe

"This feels good, or rather very good. I now have free time in my calendar and energy to work more proactively. I have time to look at tasks I should do but which I have previously been procrastinating. Your book is easy to read and funny. I am a positive and jolly time-optimist – and structure gives me the support I need to lean on."
Liv Allard, Assistant Internal Communications

"It feels wonderful and for every time that I go through your book at home or at work, I delve deeper into my new life as super-structured."
Malin Dahlquist, Project Manager Plant Engineering, Boliden Mines Technology

Published by
LID Publishing Ltd.
One Adam Street, London. WC2N 6LE

31 West 34th Street, 8th Floor, Suite 8004,
New York, NY 10001, US

info@lidpublishing.com
www.lidpublishing.com

A member of:

www.businesspublishersroundtable.com

© David Stiernholm 2017
© LID Publishing Ltd. 2017

Printed in Great Britain by TJ International
ISBN: 978-1-910649-99-2

Cover and page design: Caroline Li

DAVID STIERNHOLM

SUPER
STRUCTURED

HOW TO OVERCOME CHAOS AND WIN BACK TIME

LONDON   MONTERREY
MADRID   SHANGHAI
MEXICO CITY BOGOTA
NEW YORK   BUENOS AIRES
BARCELONA   SAN FRANCISCO

CONTENTS

ACKNOWLEDGEMENTS

A book does not write itself and the one who writes it does not do so alone. There are a few people I particularly want to extend my gratitude to:

Thank you, Micke Tegnér at my Swedish publisher Roos & Tegnér, for believing in my idea for the book, and thank you Erika Feldt, my editor for the first Swedish edition, for helping me chisel out my own personal voice and tone in the midst of all the structuring.

Thank you, Christina Bodin-Danielsson and Linda Tufvasson, for sharing your extensive knowledge regarding office environments and how to optimally design them (and what the consequences of doing so are).

Thank you, Niki Mullin at LID Publishing, for deciding to make my book available to English speakers, and thank you, Sara Taheri, for helping me make my message of structure and simplicity even more clear and communicable.

Thank you, Nicklas Bergman, my friend, for our never ceasing conversation and discussion that continues to inspire me to stretch further and further.

Thank you, Rebecka Tuma, my assistant, who has helped me so much during so many years, in an admirable way and with such a variety of things.

A big thank you to all my readers, who throughout the years have gotten in touch and shared your tools and metods that you have found or developed, and who by doing so have brought me knowledge, inspiration, joy and intoxicating delight.

And finally, thank you to my family. Life with you is the purpose of it all.

PREFACE

I recently moved into a new office. It's at the top of an old building that used to be a merchant's residence in the centre of Gothenburg. From my desk I have an excellent view of the rooftops, and on a rainy day, such as today, I can just about see the tower of Vasa Church, to the south. But I'm not sitting at my desk as I'm writing this. I prefer to do all my writing and formulating while stretched out on my beanbag, next to a somewhat overly decorated, glazed tiled stove. I turned on the recorded sound of rain that I like to listen to while I reflect and think. It then occurred to me that it's raining outside so the pleasant sounds of rain and wind are heard in the background even without headphones. Even better.

It's thanks to structure that I can enjoy this pleasant moment on the beanbag with my laptop on my knees. I know for certain that this is the right thing for me to do in the present moment. I could not possibly spend the next two hours in a better way. My one and only to-do list tells me that I have to make an important phone call during the day, but I know that I might as well do that after these two hours of writing. A quick glance at my inbox tells me that there are a few emails I should respond to before the end of the day, but I know I have time to do this later as well. There are no other items on the list that need to be dealt with immediately, everything else can wait until tomorrow. So I'm free to do what I'm doing, and I feel confident and certain that it's the right thing to do right now. This wonderful feeling of knowing with certainty that there is nothing else I should be doing is one of the reasons that I work with structure and call myself a *struktör*. Structure, to me, means having a clean conscience rather than a guilty one, being on top of things rather than lagging behind, and enjoying my work instead of worrying and agonizing.

I also know that I will not be disturbed as I have turned off my phone, shut down my email program, and closed the door. As I'm curious by nature, I have to go offline as well and hence prevent myself from accessing Facebook, Twitter, blogs, and other things one might easily drift into and get distracted by.

I know myself and I know that I enjoy checking things off, so I am running my tasks off of a to-do list I had prepared previously. Generally, I tend to prefer completing the small, concrete tasks first, but a few weeks back I reserved these two hours for writing in my calendar. This is where a tad of discipline is required, which is something I am usually not too keen on. But, if I (and you as well) am to be successful in establishing new and more advantageous habits, I need to stick to what I have decided to do. By sticking to my plans I can at least try out the idea and evaluate it.

The ceiling of my office is empty, except for the 19th century stucco work decorating it. Perhaps that's why.

I enjoy looking up at the ceiling when I'm thinking, reflecting, or pondering on something. It's a free space and by looking at it I find that I don't get distracted or lose my train of thought. No visual impressions can grab my attention and I'm allowed to think thoughts through to the very end. I work best when I am focused. That is why I've chosen to keep my desk and the surrounding space as clear and free from clutter as possible. But in spite of the world becoming increasingly digitized, there's still a continuous flow of physical paper in and out of my business. I try to store papers, notes, and publications in a structured way so that they are out of sight, but are easily accessible.

I decided to throw out all ring binders a couple of years ago after having grown tired of placing folders and loose papers in piles on my desk and on shelves in my bookcase. Now, I instead use an old Remington Rand filing cabinet I bought from a used office furniture store to hang my files.

I had the 20th century moss-green filing cabinet delivered to my office, and after giving it a good clean with a strong detergent the brass escutcheons shone once again. The four drawers are quite robust; they sound like an approaching express train when they are pulled open and they come to complete stop with a bang. I feel somewhat like a cigarette-smoking, whisky-drinking private investigator sitting in a shady office in a black-and-white movie from the 1940s. The cabinet is the only place I store my papers, even though I have fewer and fewer papers to store as time goes by. The desk is empty, which provides me with plenty of space for the materials I'm working with, but if I should need anything else, the cabinet and its contents are right next to me. I also scan much of the material I choose to keep onto my computer. These empty spaces make it easier for me to focus on my current task. My mind becomes less scattered and I feel less stressed than I used to be.

To me, the concept of structure is *only* associated with positive experiences and feelings. There are so many things I want to do and experience in my life, and being structured makes these possible in a healthy and constructive way. I have a very lucid vision of how I want my life to be and I really want to experience life, in all the ways, shapes, and forms possible. At the same time, I don't believe in working extremely hard or strenuously for a long period of time to achieve the life I want to live.

None of us know for how long we are going to live. That's why I want to enjoy life now, enjoy this very moment (as life is happening *right now*), and I really want to make use of the precious time I have with my family – my wife and my children. Being structured gives me freedom. It takes care of all the facets of life (both professionally and privately) that have to work but which I do not enjoy dealing with or keeping track of. The result is that I have more time to just be me, and express the aspects of myself which are not necessarily concerned with work. I also have more time for the tasks that really inspire me, which help me develop myself and my skills, and which constitute my greatest and most exciting challenges. Being structured allows me to feel and know that what I am doing at the moment is the right thing to do right now.

Some people have difficulties with the concept of structure. To them it is associated with rigidity, seriousness, meticulousness (just for the sake of it), bureaucracy, boredom, stuffiness, limitations, and so on. But to me structure is not at all about being strict or harsh. I see structure as a tool that makes simplicity possible. Sometimes, I'm accused of providing tips, tools and methods that "are not exactly rocket science", that are considered to be "too simplistic". And they are. In my opinion structure is all about shortcuts to a simpler and smoother life. The tips provided for being structured are simple and easy to understand; so are too their applications, and these can be useful to many different types of people.

As you might have guessed, I'm grateful to have the opportunity to work as a *struktör* and as such be able to help others improve the structure of their lives. The beauty of being structured is that even the simplest and smallest of changes often have great effects on productivity – not to mention the positive emotional and mental effects. I hope that you will find at least one tool in this book that will make your life smoother and easier.

David Stiernholm

STRUCTURE?

Structure is a broad concept. When I speak of structure I am referring to the tools, tricks, and methods that can be used to help individuals create a smoother workday.

My recommendations are concerned with the individual rather than the group – but my tips do sometimes result in improving collaboration and making it easier to work with others.

I want to help others achieve better structure in their work primarily through establishing new work habits. But most people will find that these new habits have a positive spillover effect and influence their personal lives as well.

ALL GOOD THINGS COME IN THREES

Super-structured individuals have mastered the three central areas of structure which are:

- organizing
- focusing
- automating.

These individuals are more in control of their work as, in terms of *organizing*, they have organized information, activities, projects, and papers in a carefully thought-through way. Nothing falls between the cracks and they spend as little time as possible looking for what they need. They are able to *focus* on the work at hand as they prioritize consciously, and work when and where they know they work most efficiently. They can spend adequate time on what matters to them, as they have found ways to *automate* all the tasks that simply "have to get done".

OFF TO THE PROMISED
LAND OF STRUCTURE

The journey to what I sometimes jokingly refer to as "the Shangri-La of structure" goes through these three areas, but not necessarily in that order. It is quite possible to automate part of a routine or process even if you have not organized it. But for many people it feels most natural to first organize, second, prioritize and focus on the task, and third, find as many ways as possible to work less and still get as much done but in less time. This is why I have structured the book according to these three areas.

Try to imagine a workday where you are able to work undisturbed both on the tasks you have promised to complete that day and on the long-term tasks that are not urgent. Imagine the feeling of being in control of your own time, while in communication with those you are performing tasks for and those who are in turn working for you. When you write reports, make appointments, compile notes, and so on, you will benefit from being structured and thoroughly enjoy using your templates, checklists, and scripts.

THE 31 STEPS

The book is structured as a training programme spanning 31 days. If you are not able to complete the entire programme in 31 consecutive days, this is quite all right. If you only manage to do one thing during one single day you will have accomplished more than if you had not done anything at all.

If things get hectic and you do not have time to do anything for a whole week, just pick up from where you left off. If you feel that it has been too long since you stopped following the programme, just start over. Starting over is always possible and free of charge: you can do it as many times as you like.

Personally, I repeatedly start over, especially when it comes to physical exercise. I might plan to go running three times a week, but then I catch a cold and miss a week. Instead of feeling discouraged that the plan did not work as I had intended, I just start the plan again. The point is that even if I keep starting again and again, I am keeping active and running more than if I give up completely.

Some of the 31 days in the programme are buffer days when you will not be given an assignments. These days are intended to give you space and time to catch up without being stressed by uncompleted tasks and assignments. All the people that I work with (including myself) are continuously faced with unforeseen events that can easily disrupt schedules (although one could wonder how unforeseen they really are if they occur at frequent intervals).

The 31 steps in the structure action plan need not be taken in the tempo of one assignment per day, even though this is how the programme is designed. Perhaps your situation makes it more appropriate to follow the programme over a course of 31 weeks?

When doing the programme I recommend that you choose a pace that is reasonable for you. Doing so will enable you to successfully create a better structure for your everyday life and in doing so enjoy the fruits of your efforts.

Best of luck!

STRUCTURE IS LIBERATING AND ENJOYABLE.

ORGANIZE DAY 1:
GET YOUR PLAN IN PLACE

3
Month

March 2016

Su	Mo	Tu	We	Th	Fr	Sa
28	29	1	2	3	4	5
6	7	8	9	10	11	12
13	14	15	16	17	18	19
20	21	22	23	24	25	26
27	28	29	30	31	1	2

FEB 2016

S	M	T	W	T	F	S
	1	2	3	4	5	6
7	8	9	10	11	12	13
14	15	16	17	18	19	20
21	22	23	24	25	26	27
28	29					

APR 2016

S	M	T	W	T	F	S
					1	2
3	4	5	6	7	8	9
10	11	12	13	14	15	16
17	18	19	20	21	22	23
24	25	26	27	28	29	30

Apart from giving talks and holding seminars, I help clients improve their structure individually in one-to-one sessions. They come from a wide range of industries in the private sector as well as from the public sector, but what they all have in common is that they have a lot of responsibilities, as managers, as experts, or as entrepreneurs, and their workdays are hectic. In a series of sessions, I analyse how they work and help them establish new, better structured work habits.

Yesterday I met with one of my clients for the third time. He is one of the most driven people I know and he told me about the projects he has initiated since we last met. As always I was astonished with both how ingenious and how challenging the concepts that he develops are. During our follow-up session yesterday, he told me that he felt bad for not having implemented more of the structural improvements he decided he would make. This is common with many people I meet and work with. They are highly motivated to address their situation at work and to make it more sustainable, but for some reason they don't follow through on what they initially intend to do and the ambitious pace they set for themselves. And the longer they wait, the heavier their conscience grows, and the opportunities to actually make the changes they wanted to make are lost.

To address this, my client and I stood in front of a whiteboard and drew a timeline starting from today and ending in two months' time. We considered the structural improvements as projects like all others and with that things got moving. We defined everything that needs to be done as concrete to-do tasks and even scheduled time in his crowded calendar for doing those tasks. The concrete plan creates the right prerequisites to actually implement the improvements.

Welcome to Day 1 in the training programme for creating better structure. You have 31 tasks ahead of you to do during 31 days. It will take some time – not much, but nonetheless it will require commitment.

TASK

Improving your habits at work should be regarded as a project, just like any other project you are responsible for completing. Personally I am very restrictive when it comes to scheduling time beforehand for doing particular tasks, as at the time of doing the scheduling I cannot possibly know what tasks I will need to prioritize on any given day. But, if you wish to follow through with this endeavour, you might as well reserve the time required now so that you don't back down because of a lack of it later.

So, your first task is to decide on 31 half-hour time slots when you will work on your *structure* project. Make it easy for yourself by creating recurring *structure meetings* with yourself, and ensure that these meetings occur at the same time every day. If your calendar is already nearly full, then simply book these half-hour meetings with yourself wherever there is time. In order to do some of these tasks, you will need to be physically present in your office, but having access to your computer will suffice for most tasks.

It may be that some of your scheduled structure meetings collide with other more important events. In these instances, rather than removing it completely you should change the time of that specific structure meeting.

We are all different and have different needs and the 31-day programme is flexible so that you can use it in a way that suits you. Depending on what you wish to improve in your work and life, you can choose to spend a little extra time and effort on various aspects of the programme.

So, what are your workdays like? Do you feel that:

- you often remember tasks being due before the end of the day just before leaving the office, and have to work overtime to finish them? If so, mark the half-hour you have reserved for Day 25 of the programme as extra important, as it will help you with this particular tendency.

- you have a desk that looks like World War III, and you easily get distracted by all the things you repeatedly catch a glimpse of (and which are irrelevant to what you are currently working on) while sitting by your desk? If so, mark the half-hour on Day 8 as extra important.

- you find it difficult to get an overview of all your engagements, projects, and tasks, as you write down all the things you need to do in several places? Then mark the half-hour you have reserved for Day 2 as extra important.

- you find it hard to concentrate on the task in front of you as you continually get disturbed and interrupted? If so, mark the half-hour for Day 16 as extra important.

- you have too much to do and want to get better at prioritizing? Then mark the half-hour of Day 11 as extra important.

- smaller tasks take so much of your time that you do not have time to work on the more extensive, long-terms tasks until late on the night before the deadline? If that is often the case, then mark the half-hour of Day 17 as extra important.

REWARD

The second thing I want you to do before you start, is to find a way to reward yourself as you progress through the programme. If you enjoy sweets, buy a bag of something you are particularly fond of and treat yourself with a sweet for every task you complete. If you have longed for some gadget or thing that you do not actually need or think you can afford, divide the price by 31 and give yourself a 1/31 token every time you have completed a task. Purchase a bag of cotton pulp balls in an arts and crafts shop (in my town that store is called "The Therapy House" and it is filled to the brim with yarns, chenille stems, figures for wood crafts and paint), and line up a row of balls on your windowsill one by one as you complete the tasks. Or, draw a line on the whiteboard as you do a task, as if you were a prisoner counting off the days until your release. One of my clients got a box of extra-large matches and wrote a sub-goal on every one of them. For every goal she at-tained, she lit the match and enjoyed the accomplishment of having successfully finished while the match burned out.

There are of course infinite ways to reward yourself. If you think of some other way, feel free to email me at super@stiernholm.com and tell me. I am all ears and I'm curious to hear what you come up with.

Do all the above and reward yourself for doing so with the reward you chose.

ORGANIZE DAY 2:

CHOOSE YOUR TOOL

TO DO LIST

- ☐ meeting
- ☐ email
- ☐ phone call

{ Not until we have all our **to-do tasks** in one place can we get an overview. }

Most people I meet through my work as a *struktör* produce notes on what they have to do and keep these in several different places. With only a few exceptions to this rule, I would say that this is a common mistake to make. Having many places where to look for what to do next can make life so much more difficult than it needs to be.

You may receive a great number of emails, and choose to mark those that you can't answer immediately, as well as those that require action (other than sending another email), with flags or stars. Perhaps you even have a to-do folder with all the emails you need to attend to, but just not right now. Other times you simply mark the emails as "unread" to signal to yourself that you need to get back to them at some point when you have more time.

You might have the habit of grabbing a sheet of paper and jotting down what is on your mind, so that you don't forget to do it later. And you also have all the little notes, where you have scribbled down what you discussed on the phone with a client a few minutes ago, and these are spread out all over your desk. With the volume of new technology available, you may have found yourself a clever app for your phone where you choose to add yet another few tasks. Perhaps the app is called "ToDo". And when you had lunch at that nice, recently opened restaurant the other day, a colleague suggested an app that is supposedly much better, named "2Do". Or was it "To Do", or perhaps "Toodledo"? Anyhow, you have now downloaded these too.

An important report is due on Thursday and so that you do not forget about it, you have created a "send the report" entry in your calendar on the day that it's due. Just in case you forget, you turn the calendar reminder on, to alert you a few hours before the deadline, so your phone will notify you as well.

This morning you had a meeting concerning a new project, and you were asked to make a few calls after it was over. You made notes of the new task on a notepad you always bring to meetings, and placed the paper with notes in the in tray on your desk, titled "To do". This is where you usually put the incoming papers that need attending to. You place the most urgent papers at an angle so that they will be sure to catch your attention later. But, you keep all the things you need to do during the day in your head, as you do not want to waste time writing them down. And often you actually remember at least most of the tasks you need to do!

You are not only responsible for your own projects, but also participate in several external projects and collaborations as well. Your clients handle their projects in a virtual project room where the project plans are located, and where you can see who is responsible for what. But the advertising agency you use has set up their project on an American web service.

And today, in spite of it being a sunny day, you have simply had it. It's all just too much. You do not know where to start or what to start with. When you look up from your desk, you happen to spot that flyer from head office that you had pinned to your noticeboard so you would not forget to summon the staff for a meeting regarding its contents.

Unfortunately, this is very common situation for many people. You will find that the more places you spread your notes on what you need to do, the harder it will be to identify what you need to focus on right now. Not until all your to-do tasks are gathered or consolidated in one place will you be able to get an overview of everything that requires your time. And it will not be until you've done this that you'll be able to prioritize your tasks accurately while being certain that you are not missing anything crucial or urgent.

I personally began seriously using lists in my work in 1999 when I built my first list tool in the data-base software Microsoft Access. At the time I had several roles in the organization I was working in, with several individuals in the company giving me assignments, many projects of all sizes active simultaneously, a number of deadlines, and to top that off, not a great deal of time to do it all in. In my list program, which I thought appropriate to name "Structure.mdb", I stored everything I had to do, and I was able to alter the list to find the right thing to do from one moment to the next by using all kinds of categories.

When David Allen's well-known book *Getting Things Done* (2001) came out a couple of years later, I felt reassured that my working methods were sensible and that I was not the only one finding to-do lists useful. Having said this, it was neither Allen nor myself who invented the concept of a "to-do list". Through the ages, writing lists has been a simple way for people to keep a track of everything that has to be done. An illustrative example is that according to historian Toby Lester in his book *Da Vinci's Ghost: Genius, Obsession, and How Leonardo Created the World in His Own Image* (2012), Leonardo Da Vinci always kept a notebook containing a to-do list in his belt. And this is for a good reason as, according to a study by Masicampo and Baumeister in 2011, an individual can only fully focus on the right task at the right time when a list and/or a plan is prepared containing all of their tasks. So it is very likely that you will not be able to relax until you have consolidated all of your to-do tasks into one single place. You will find that simply priceless.

TASK

1. Get yourself a blank sheet of paper.

2. Write down all the things you have to do as they come to your mind at the moment. Try to mostly include work-related tasks, but if you think of important tasks that concern your private life, write them down as well. Start with what you have to do today, this week, and so on, and continue as far ahead in time as you feel is relevant and helpful. If you for instance know that you always start working on the budget in October, then write that down.

3. Make a decision and determine where you will keep all your to-do tasks from now on. Most people opt for a digital tool, such as Outlook, a web service, or an app of some kind. I built my very own digital to-do list tool in a database application back in 1999, but I have now left that one far behind. If you follow the URL or QR code below you will see my suggestions for five of the best digital to-do list tools. But do bear in mind that this is a continuously developing area, and although my suggestions may be the best right now, this may only be so for a while.

www.superstructured.com/todo-list-tools

If you prefer a physical tool instead of a digital one, then here are some ideas:

Pen and paper. A pen and a paper are always more or less easily accessible. They always work (if the pen is out of ink, you will soon locate one that works), they never crash, you don't have to log into any kind of system to have access to them, and they are easy to take anywhere. On the other hand, it is difficult to sort the tasks and it can be tricky to hide those that you are not prioritizing at any one time, which you preferably should get out of your sight. If you find a way to easily indicate what project a task is a part of, and you do not have to spend too much time rewriting the list – because it has become too messy – then pen and paper could be an excellent choice.

Notepad. You may find that you can fit many tasks into a notepad over time, and that it's easy to keep a bank of to-do tasks in one place. As you probably cannot fold the notepad up and put it in your pocket as easily as a piece of paper, it is not as portable. And it can be tempting to confuse to-do tasks with other random notes, sketches, and phone numbers that might end up in the note-pad unintentionally. If they do, it gets difficult to maintain a comprehensive overview of the list. But, as long as you can refine and dedicate the notepad to your to-do tasks alone, you will find it to be a satisfying tool as well.

Index cards. Fifteen shiny, playing-card sized cards joined together by a document clip are usually called index cards (or "Hipster PDA", as the productivity writer Merlin Mann, the creator of the concept "Zero Inbox", has named them). They are easy to take everywhere and you can take them out of your pocket quickly when you need to make a note. The index cards will not break if you drop them and the tasks are easier to group than if you write your list on regular paper. However, just like the physical tools mentioned above, they are not very convenient if we should need to make a back-up – then we might be in for a lot of writing by hand. But if you always keep a stack of fresh cards in the pile, and make sure to take them wherever you go without even thinking about it, then they constitute a most excellent tool.

A notebook divided by tabs. If you want a more robust but still portable tool for your tasks, a notebook can be the tool for you. It is important that you keep it clean from other content though, so that you can distinguish your to-do tasks from ideas, sketches, and other notes.

If you wish to group the tasks by project or some other categorization that you consider relevant, such as how much time each one takes to complete, then cut tabs into the pages or paste tabs to mark out the different sections. By doing this you will be able to get to the section you are looking for by just opening the notebook at the right tab.

Just as with the other physical tools, you may be tempted to process the tasks that arise via email separately. This avoids having to write out follow-up responses to emails as a separate task. But at the same time, if you do not write down all of your tasks in one place, you run the risk of ending up with one "regular" to-do list in the notebook and one parallel, unofficial, to-do list consisting of all the emails you have marked to do something with or follow-up on. If you get a notebook that you enjoy writing in, that is easy to take everywhere and can be laid open on your desk without you having to hold it open, then this might be a good tool for you.

Sticky notes. From time to time, even I have been guilty of nagging people about sticky notes pasted on to computer screens, keyboards, wall calendars, and more or less everywhere in offices. But perhaps I'm being a bit unfair. A young entrepreneur, who runs three growing businesses (and who has surely started more since I last spoke to him) kept track of everything he needed to do with an intricate sticky note system he had devised. He pasted the notes in a matrix on his desk according to what business they concerned and when the tasks needed to be done. The different colours represented different types of tasks.

So, it is possible to work in a structured way using sticky notes as well. You can scribble something on them quickly and easily, it feels great to crumple them up and throw them away once the task is done, and they provide an excellent overview. They can, however, be impractical if you travel a lot for work, and they're not ideal for use in open offices as colleagues can easily get an overview of your tasks and thus see when you intend to do the particular tasks they asked you to do.

But if you can find a systemized way to organize and place your sticky notes, so that you don't paste notes wherever there is space, and if you only move within a reasonably small perimeter in your office (so that you do not have to take your to-do list with you), then sticky notes can be an incredibly smart, fast, and easy tool to use.

If you are to rely on your written to-do list as your only tool for keeping track of what you have to do, note that the physical, paper-based tools have a disadvantage as they are sometimes lost or find their way accidentally into the laundry if left in a pocket.

GAIN

If you can gather all your notes on the tasks you have to do in a single location, you will be able to determine which task is the right one to do next, much faster. You'll find that you no longer stumble upon old notes about something you should have done ages ago. You can rest assured that you will remember to really do what you promise others. And you no longer have to work overtime because of remembering much too late that you should have done something earlier during the day.

REWARD

If you chose what tool to use for your to-do list, give yourself a reward. It does not have to be the ultimate tool that you use from here to eternity, but at least a tool that is good enough for now and for the foreseeable future.

BEFORE WE PART FOR TODAY

One more thing: if you follow this book and the programme it contains, in about a week you will get the opportunity to clarify to yourself the goals you are striving toward which will influence how you prioritize your tasks.

Do you know what goals you are aiming to achieve this year? If not, schedule a meeting with your boss to discuss this matter, preferably sometime in the coming week, and if not in person, then at least over the phone.

"Let me tell you the secret that has led me to my goal.
My strength lies solely in my tenacity."
Louis Pasteur (1822–1895)

ORGANIZE DAY 3:

CONSOLIDATE YOUR TASKS

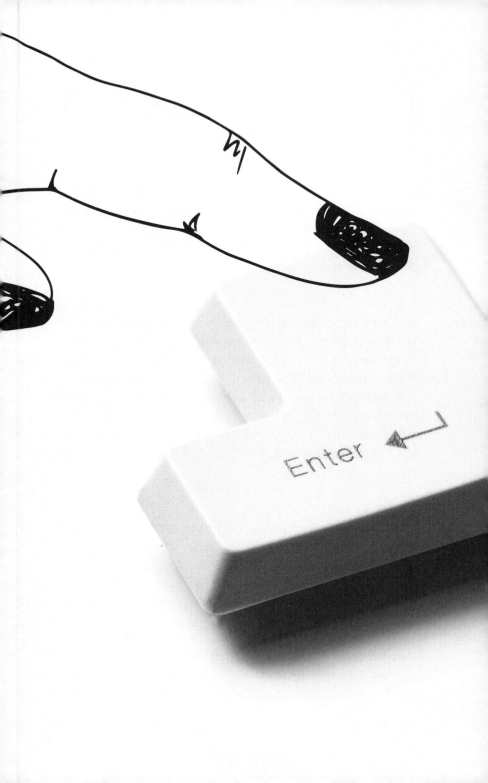

{ Do not fall into the trap of abstraction –
formulate the tasks concretely
and detailed. }

A few years ago, I helped an entrepreneur in the fashion industry with her structure; both her personal structure and her structure at work. She was originally a midwife and at one point while we were talking about to-do tasks, she told me the following story.

One day a mother-to-be, who happened to have an unusual rash on her stomach, visited her at the midwife's office. My client thought, "We really should look into that," wrote "Important! Belly!" on a sticky note and pasted it on the front of the patient's medical record. After a few days she found that patient's record in one of the piles on her desk. Since writing the note she had seen a number of other patients and now she couldn't recollect what she'd meant by her note. As you might have guessed, she sees her fair share of bellies in her line of work.

TASK

Yesterday, you gathered all of the to-do tasks you could think of into a single location, and you chose a tool you can use to consolidate these going forward.

Today, it is time to enter your tasks into the tool you have selected.

They say that "The devil's in the detail," and this is certainly true for formulating to-do tasks. If you define a task too broadly, you will still have to keep the details and the various steps involved in the tasks in your head in order to complete it and check it off your list.

Sometimes it may seem unnecessary to define the first step required to begin a task, but by defining the subsequent steps and not the first you will be none the wiser about where to actually begin.

Sometimes you may think that it is too much work to write out full sentences, and end up formulating the task ambiguously. Although this saves time initially, when reviewing your list later you may find that you have no idea what the note means.

Do not fall into the trap of the abstract – formulate the details of the tasks concretely and thoroughly. Define them in such detail that you will be able to do them in one go, or at least during the course of a day. If you first have to do one thing and then another before you can check a to-do task off the list, then divide it into two separate tasks instead. Yes, you will have more to-do tasks, and yes, they will take slightly longer to write down, but on the other hand you will create a list that you can feel safe with. You will no longer have to remember steps and segments of each to-do task that are not on the to-do list.

Make sure that each to-do task contains a verb, as this will ensure that you produce a list of tasks that are of a reasonable size. If you just write "the porch", you will definitely be more prone to postponing what needs to be done compared with writing "buy screws for the porch". Beware of verbs such as "fix" or "make sure that" and other ambiguous descriptions of what you intend to do: these references could potentially hide an entire project in vague phrasing.

If you have chosen a digital tool for your to-do list, I am guessing that there are a lot of different details to fill out, for instance categories, priority, starting date, due date, date for reminder, time requirement, and probably many more. As you enter your tasks into the digital tool you have chosen, make the entry as simple and as relevant as possible. The more boxes and settings you choose to fill out, the more options you will be presented with and the longer it will take. What matters most at this first stage is the practice of entering all of the tasks into the tool. You can always complement each task by adding more information later when everything is in place.

If you have chosen a notebook divided by tabs as your to-do list tool, or some other physical tool where you want to group the tasks by tab dividers or something else, I would recommend you to jump to Day 5 now, read that section (and do the accompanying task), and then come back here to Day 3. (Day 5 looks at categorizing to-do tasks, and if you use a physical tool it is preferable that you have decided on what categories to use before you set up your to-do list.)

Use the method below for whichever physical or digital tool you have chosen.

So, for today:

1. Start by entering the tasks you have to do today.

2. Then add the tasks you need to complete this week, this month, the next few months, or by the end of the year.

3. Go through the notepad that you usually take to meetings and add any tasks you find among these notes.

4. Go through any notes lying around on your desk and add any tasks that might be written on these.

5. Go through any pictures, papers, or flyers you have posted on your walls and enter any to-do tasks they remind you of.

6. Think through all the projects you are involved in and add any tasks you are responsible for doing.

7. Flip through all the piles of paper you have in your office and gather any to-do tasks that might lurk in these. You do not have to sort through the piles now as we will deal with them another day. The important thing right now is just to sift out any tasks that might be hiding there, so that nothing gets forgotten past its due date, buried deep in a pile.

8. Finally, go through the emails you have in your email inbox, both those you received recently and those you have left there and planned to deal with at some point. Instead of using the email inbox as an ambiguous ad hoc list, create to-do tasks out of anything you have to do regarding the emails and their content. Not until you have done this final step will you truly have gathered all of your to-do tasks in a single location.

REWARD
When you have entered all your to-do tasks into your to-do list and there are none left behind elsewhere, give yourself a generous reward of the kind you chose earlier. I am aware of that this task is a large one and for some it takes more than a calendar day, so let me here and now give you a pat on the back across time and space.

ORGANIZE DAY 4:

TAKE TIME TO RECAP

{   Expect the unexpected.   }

Sometimes things just do not turn out as planned. We intend to make a change and create an ambitious plan for doing so. But then something unforeseen throws us off our course. Tasks previously considered to be of high priority may suddenly no longer be as important as a newer, more urgent task.

Many people who wish to improve on their structure often want to jump-start the structuring process. But, when unexpected events happen (and unexpected things can happen all the time), their schedule and plan get disrupted. They then come to the conclusion that their work situation is simply impossible to change, and that their particular case is exceptionally hopeless. They feel discouraged instead of motivated, which is a shame. So, to avoid having plans derailed, you should do your best to expect the unexpected. This is why I am giving you a buffer day today. You will not be given a new task today, but instead an opportunity to get back on track if you have fallen behind with any of the previous tasks.

If you want to, and feel that you are on track with the programme, then come with me to a lunch I had with a business acquaintance a sunny Monday a few years ago. I remember that we were sitting at an Asian restaurant in Gothenburg enjoying the sunshine. As I find it fascinating to hear of other people's perspectives on my topic, I asked her: "What is structure to you?" My acquaintance, Amanda, answered: "Structure is knowing; knowing what you have to do and when you have to do it by, where you have everything you need, and what is important." And I could not agree with her more. With good structure you do not have to hesitate, you can feel safe, and you can relax.

ORGANIZE DAY 5:
CREATE YOUR CATEGORIES

{ Categorize **to-do tasks**. }

A couple of years ago I spent a few cold days in a city in the north of Sweden. I had the pleasure of holding a course for three groups of managers on structure and an efficient to-do list. When I spoke about the value of just having one to-do list containing all the tasks that take no longer than a workday to complete, one of the managers threw his hands in the air and exclaimed "But that is completely unreasonable! If I were to have just one long list with everything – everything – that I have to do, I would feel exhausted just looking at it!" I have to say that I agreed with him. But luckily it's quite rare – if ever at all – for you to have to view the entire list at once. That will not be the case if you are working with good structure. By grouping the tasks together in a way that makes sense to you, you can, and you will only need to view a selection of tasks that are relevant at that moment. Rather than seeing all the 168 items on your list, you get an overview of the 12 you wish to complete right now.

By categorizing you will not get distracted by seeing the tasks that you are not interested in dealing with right now, and it will be easier to concentrate on the task ahead.

You may find that at certain times you only want to view the tasks belonging to a certain project, but right now you want an overview of the tasks you can do while you are on the train, as the on-board internet connection proves to be much more stable than anticipated. At another time you may want to see only the tasks you can do while waiting for a colleague who just called to say he will be 15 minutes late for a meeting.

This is why you should categorize to-do tasks on your to-do list. The list opposite suggests some useful considerations for putting tasks into categories:

- What project is the task a part of?
  Often, plenty of our to-do tasks are parts of a project (in the classic sense) or a larger task (that we usually do not think of as a project, but that consists of many smaller steps and that takes longer than a workday to complete). When you want to focus entirely on moving forward on one particular project the next hour, this categorization lets you see only the to-do tasks that concern that project.

- Who are you doing the task for?
  This can help you to see what tasks you need to complete before you have that meeting pencilled in for later in the afternoon.

- Where do you need to physically be in order to do the task?
  All tasks are not the same and each may need a different location. Think about where each task can be most efficiently completed: in the office, at home, while you are out running errands, in the lab, in the storage space, in building C, in the hotel room, in the car, or at the company office located in another city?

- What tool or system do you need to complete the task?
  The computer, the phone, the internet, the business system, or some other program or device.

- What discussions do you need to have for the to-do task? This will help you to park the things that you want to bring up during the next meeting in advance. You will then easily find the issues you wanted to bring up while preparing for the meeting in question.

- How much time will the task take to complete? Is it 5 minutes, 15 minutes, 30 minutes, or an hour?

- What state of mind should you be in to perform the task? Is this something for which you need to have all your wits about you to do or could you do the simple, somewhat boring task when you are tired and unfocused?

- What type of environment do you need to be in to successfully complete the task? A business acquaintance of mine categorizes certain tasks as "peace and quiet". She works on this category of task on mornings when she gets to work an hour before everyone else: when the office is peaceful and quiet.

- When does the task need to be completed by? The due date can itself be regarded as a category, and if tasks have been tagged with a deadline, we can allow the list to only display tasks due today.

You can choose to select by just using one category at a time, or you could use several simultaneously. Perhaps you want to for instance only see the short 5-minute tasks that are on your list and which you could do while on the plane later today. But be careful. If you are not used to categorizing your to-do tasks, then just choose one way to categorize your to-do tasks, and then add more categories and simultaneous categorizations gradually. Otherwise you will perceive this method as difficult and complicated, and go back to remembering things instead of writing them down (as "it's just faster that way").

In most, if not all, digital to-do list tools you can categorize tasks by checking a category box, using labels, or using tags. If your to-do list is in a physical format, you have several options: you can choose to denote categories by using symbols which you write before every to-do task, you can split your notebook into sections representing the different categories by using tabs or dividers, or you can indicate the categories by highlighting tasks using different coloured highlighters.

TASK

1. Choose a way to categorize to-do tasks. What categories will you initially use? Select a few, say four or five different categories, and add more as you go along. Learn how to use categorization in an efficient way.

2. Create categories for the to-do tasks on your one and only to-do list. You will experience the true meaning and benefits of this method only when all tasks have been categorized. Otherwise you will need to look in two or more different places to determine what task to do next – among the to-do tasks that have been categorized and those that have not.

3. Now test it out by selecting and viewing one of your categories. Notice how much easier it is to get a grasp of your list when you don't have to view all the items it contains at the same time.

GAIN

Let us say you divide your list by using five categories. Every time you browse your list for things to do by a particular category, it will only take a fifth of the time it would have otherwise taken. As you are only viewing one category at a time, you will be able to deduce what you can and what you should be doing right now.

If you used to look through your to-do list five times a day and it approximately took a minute every time, you will have gained four minutes per day, which is approximately 17 hours in a year. But these extra hours gained are nothing compared with no longer constantly feeling scattered, distracted, and stressed by seeing all the things you have to do at some point, but are unable to attend to right now. Being able to focus on fewer things while feeling that you have got everything else under control too, is priceless.

REWARD

When you have assigned categories to all your tasks, set your to-do list (if it is digital – otherwise flip to the right page or tab) to display only the tasks you can do right now or which are relevant to the system or context you are currently working in. Enjoy having the opportunity to choose from only a few, but from the right tasks. Feel free getting started with the task you feel most like doing, and rest assured that there is nothing else you ought to be doing right now. Even if that in itself is reward enough, reward yourself in the way you chose earlier.

ORGANIZE DAY 6:

FORM AN OVERVIEW

{ Create an overview for all your
more extensive tasks and projects. }

"Oh, well, I keep that in my head. Or on the notes I have all around here. Oh, and in my email inbox. Well, that's about it," my client answered when I asked him how he keeps track of all the detailed tasks he has to do. I asked him if he used a tool to keep track of all his to-do tasks, and when he replied "Sure, we have a project management tool for that," we had a look at it. And indeed, the project management tool contained all the different phases of the project and their separate parts. But I thought it looked a little abstract and vague, so I asked him how long it takes him to do the tasks named "Action", which constituted the smallest unit in the project management tool. The answer was one to two months. And in response to this answer came my next query. I asked him what his perspective was on the next thing he needs to do, and how he remembers all the things he needs for each project, such as sending emails, calling people, summarizing things, and so on. He had a very clear plan of what steps to take in the project and where it was heading, but it was all at a very high level. You can liken it to a fire escape that ends a few metres above the ground. If you are on the ground, wanting to climb it, you have nothing to help you to get started moving up the ladder. Essentially, the clearly defined steps begin too far above your head.

When you wrote your complete to-do list during Day 3, did you end up with a long or a short list? Some people have a remarkably short list considering that they always have so much to do. However, many of the tasks they have to complete take more than a day to finish. And these larger tasks normally consist of many smaller tasks. This could be, e.g. a project, which involves communications with many potential clients, or many assignments that need completing, or problems that need to be solved, cases that still need attending to, and much more. By using a shortlist, where the tasks are phrased in very general terms, then the list is actually quite unhelpful. You'll find that you have work, work, and more work, but it takes forever to cross anything off the list. You continue to check and send emails, make calls, gather people for meetings, attend meetings, write, report, design, and so on, until ultimately you get to tick the tasks off the list, in your head.

A short to-do list then turns out to be more of an overview of the extensive tasks and initiatives you are responsible for rather than a list of the tasks you have to do. Such an overview is definitely valuable, but it needs to be separated from the actual to-do list.

TASK

Create an overview of all the more extensive tasks and projects you are responsible for. Do this:

1. Decide where you will keep your overview. A few typical solutions are:
   - a list in a word processing document
   - a spreadsheet where every project can be divided into subprojects
   - a mind-map in some digital tool
   - a pin board in your office
   - a digital Kanban board where you collaborate with others
   - a separate list in the tool you have chosen for your to-do tasks.

2. Go through your to-do list and transfer all tasks that take longer than a day to complete to the project overview.

3. Add any other larger things, tasks or projects you are responsible for doing. Now is not the time to judge how important or business-related the project is. If it is something you want to work on and that takes several steps to complete, it is worth adding it to your overview.

4. Go through the overview and develop a concrete step for each and every one of the initiatives you have listed, these could be either something you will need to do or something you are waiting for from someone else. Add these steps to your to-do list (if they are not already there).

GAIN

If you have created an overview and defined the next step to take regarding all your currently active projects, you can be sure that nothing gets forgotten or falls between two stools, and that everything will now move at least one step forward.

REWARD

If you cannot think of any more projects when browsing through your overview (being sure to include the project of improving your structure as well), and you have defined the next step for every project, reward yourself in the way you previously determined you would.

And finally, simply enjoy having taken yet another step toward making your workdays structured.

Well done!

ORGANIZE DAY 7:

HUNT OUT THE MILLSTONES

{ # What is the first, smallest step? }

A to-do list that is constantly transforming and reforming, even though it happens to be quite long, is nice to have. By checking tasks off your list regularly, you'll get to experience the rush of having taken yet another step and having accomplished something from your to-do list. But, most people have tasks that tend to remain on the list day in and day out, week after week, and sometimes even months on end. I refer to these tasks that remain seemingly forever on the list, fermenting and brewing frustration, as "millstones" around our necks that weigh us down. They are downright awful. Every time you see these uncompleted on your list, you may feel a bit disheartened. The longer you put these off, the harder it is to get started.

Not too long ago I coordinated an exercise with a large group where the participants were asked to select a millstone each from their list and think about what the first step to get going again could be. One man raised his hand and said "My first step is to sign in to the system." That is a small step indeed. And, as it so happens, one universal trick for getting rid of a metaphorical millstone is to think of the first, smallest little step that can be taken to get the task or project moving again. Do not hesitate to define an almost ridiculously small step like the example above. You are stuck and need to get moving again. When that is the case, any step taken is progress. A concrete way to get going is to move the millstone to your overview of all your major tasks, projects or areas of responsibility, and then define the first step as a concrete to-do task that you add to your to-do list. If you will need to take several steps to complete the task we can regard it as a small project.

Define the next step, one after another, as you gradually complete the task.

TASK

1. Skim through your to-do list and keep an eye out for "millstones". They might be tasks you have defined too broadly (so that they require more work than you have time for in a day). They can be tasks that in themselves are quite small, but tasks that for some reason you have been putting off doing.

2. Transfer the millstone onto your overview of major tasks and projects.

3. For every millstone, formulate the next possible step as a to-do task. Make it so small that you almost do not want to write it on your to-do list. Then it will be really easy to do it, and you will soon be on your way with the procrastinated project or task, feeling boosted and motivated (which is a much nicer sensation than feeling stuck and passive).

4. If you have many millstones and you feel disappointed when you see them, make the decision to tackle one per day. Every morning, choose which one of the millstones you will progress with that day. If you should feel like taking more steps than that initial one regarding the millstone of the day, then by all means, go for it.

GAIN

If you make it a habit to divide the millstones that get stuck on your list into smaller steps, you'll start tackling them sooner and you'll find that you are completing more of the things you are responsible for. You'll feel like a real "doer" instead of feeling disappointed in yourself every time you browse through the list and find these incomplete to-do tasks. Otherwise you will not want to browse through your list very often, and this may in itself initiate a negative spiral of deteriorating structure.

REWARD

If you no longer have any millstones left on your to-do list and if you have defined a next step for each new project, you should reward yourself in the manner you chose on the first day of the programme.

ORGANIZE DAY 8:

GET STUCK IN

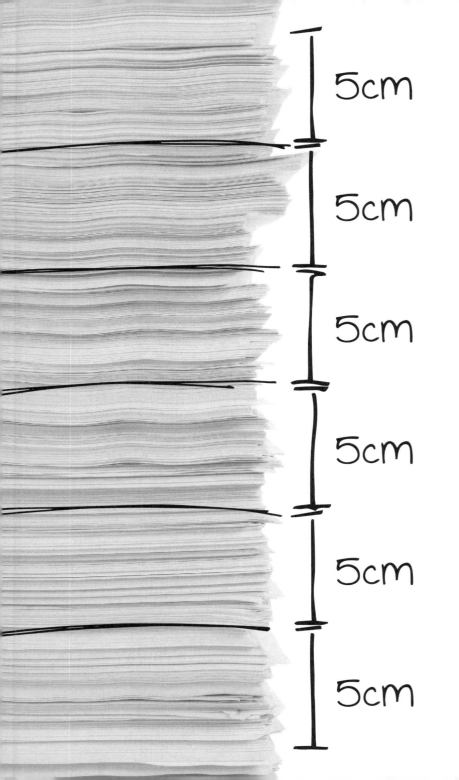

{ What if the things we see on our walls
when we look up from our desk
are images and texts that inspire us? }

Many times when I visit clients and business acquaintances in their offices, they say things such as "You'll have to excuse the mess. I should have cleaned it up before you came," and make a dis-heartened, sweeping gesture toward the room at large.

I always feel bad that for no good reason they are not happy with their environment when meeting with me, because I'm really not one to judge. But even worse, it worries me that they spend their workdays surrounded by clutter and things that they are not comfortable with, things which do not energize or inspire them. I understand that it can be nice to have the papers you need in easy reach, but the inclination to encour-age this comfort tends to only create more piles of paper. And if we have created two piles, a third will soon have appeared, and before we know it, the entire desk is covered in temporary piles of materials.

The problem with piles of paper is not only the space they require, in that the more piles you have, the less space you have for whatever you are working on right now. The issue is, at its core, actually more about safety and quality. You can probably get rather good at navigating through all your piles, heaps, and mounds of paper, but what happens if you get sick and a colleague needs to locate the project material that you think you know the exact location of? The most com-mon consequence of working among piles is that you are dis-tracted. When you are deeply concentrated on the task you really don't need to raise your eyes for a moment and catch a glimpse of some notes on the top of the pile on your left. Then suddenly you remember that you promised to call that person you met last week, and immediately you have lost all concentration and have to try to refocus on the task you were in the middle of.

What if you keep all the surfaces surrounding you free from clutter, so that you can let your gaze and thoughts wander freely without catching sight of and being reminded of things that distract you? Or, what if the things you see as your eyes sweep across the room are images and texts that inspire you and make it easier for you to complete the tasks you are working on, rather than scatter your attention?

You'll find that the more places you use to store papers in, the easier it becomes for piles to form there and throughout the entire office. If you use many different storage places to choose between (such as binders, magazine files, inboxes, hanging file folders, piles, and so on), you'll not be entirely sure that you'll find a document later when you need it. When the number of storage options increases, so does your concern for not finding the material again, and you simply won't dare to put it away. You need to feel safe and in control, hence you'll place documents where you can easily see them – at the top of a pile or in an empty space on the desk.

And then there are the digital files. New solutions for digital document management are constantly being launched, both for larger organizations and for individual users. Each one is brilliant in their own way. They have indexes, you can use tags, they are available in the cloud, you can share documents with others, working on the same document simultaneously in different parts of the world, you can check in and check out, synchronize to all kinds of devices and places, categorize, filter, and selectively view. You can save local files on your laptop, place them in a shared file server, in your own area on the shared file server, in the document management system, and in the document area of the project management portal. You can upload files to the cloud service and create completely new files in another service, where the documents do not ever get saved on your own computer. With the intention of having relevant documents easily accessible, some people even save so many of them on their computer desktop that they can no longer see their own children! (Assuming that they've used a picture of them as their desktop background.) But, even if the documents are digital, by spreading the documents in many different places you are making things significantly more difficult for yourself. By choosing to store your documents in only a few places, you'll find it easier to store them away in the first place, and you'll find it easier and faster to locate them.

TASK

Have a look at where you store your documents and papers. Here are some possible locations.

- piles on the desk
- magazine files
- inboxes
- hanging file folders
- piles in the bookcase
- piles on the bookcase
- plastic bag behind the door
- unopened removals box

- the predecessor's binders that you need to go through when you have time
- document management system for digital files
- the computer desktop
- the web-based project space
- locally on your hard drive
- the shared file server
- the old shared file server that you are no longer supposed to use
- USB sticks
- a portable, external hard drive
- in a cloud-based service (as this book is written, a few relevant examples are Drop-box, Google Drive, OneDrive, Box, or iCloud, but it is possible that when you are holding this book in your hand, they are already old)
- your personal space on the shared server
- in your email inbox
- in your smartphone
- any other place where you like to squirrel things away

You can tackle this!

1. Decide on which place or location you want to get rid of. Even if having a few places is preferable, it will still make a big difference if you manage to get rid of at least one of all the locations you currently use.

2. To make progress toward using only a few storage places, clean out three "units" of what-ever you are storing in the place you have chosen to get rid of. By a unit I mean a paper, a digital document, a brochure, a report, or something else.

For every unit, ask yourself: "Is there a next step associated with this material?" If so, create a to-do task describing that step (unless it is already on your to-do list). Then ask yourself: "Can I throw it out?" If the answer is yes, then do so. If not, file it away in the new designated place where it belongs from now on.

3. I am guessing that you have not cleared the storage place you want to rid yourself of completely yet and that there are still a few documents to go through. Cleaning it out and sorting it all into new locations is to be regarded as a project, and therefore belongs on your overview of major tasks and projects. Define a project along the lines of: "Get rid of desk trays" or "Transfer all notes from the phone". Decide what the next step ought to be and add it as a to-do task to your list. If you think you will need it, schedule time in your calendar when you perform this particular next step. Consider what tempo you think will be realistic to keep. How much will you have time and energy for? One tab every week? 5cm off the top of a pile of paper per day?

Let's say you choose to get rid of 5cm. When the time comes: measure 5cm of the pile. Lift up the top 5cm and insert a coloured sheet of paper on to the top of the remaining pile so that it becomes clear what you'll work with today. This will give you a clear goal; you will work until only the dividing paper is at the top of the pile. Process the 5cm. When you reach the coloured paper, measure up another 5cm and stick the coloured sheet in at the bottom of these. If it turns out that you feel like and you have time to process the next 5cm straight away instead of waiting until tomorrow, then go right ahead and continue processing.

GAIN

If you get rid of all the piles you have on your desk, you will be less distracted when you really need to concentrate. If you save digital files in fewer places, you will not have to get distracted by always searching for them. The *Harvard Business Review* covered a study (Apgar, 2000) which showed that out of an average 8-hour workday, approximately 70 minutes a day were lost and wasted because of distractions. If you can decrease that time-loss by only a tenth (according to the study, 7 minutes per day), this is equivalent of 3.5 full workdays in a year. Of course you will not magically have an extra 3.5 empty days in your calendar, but during those seven minutes you can make that extra call, have that little break you definitely need, or exert a little extra effort when working on a task so that the quality of what you deliver becomes even higher.

REWARD

If you clean out three units and make a simple plan of how and when you are going to clean out the rest, then reward yourself in your favourite way. If you manage to get rid of the place you want to remove entirely, then reward yourself a little extra.

ORGANIZE DAY 9:

TAKE YOUR TIME

{ Good structure is the prerequisite
for living the life I lead. }

Today I am giving you another buffer day. If you have time and feel like it, read about how good structure gives my client Lasse more time to be who he is and who he wants to be.

Lasse is a true enthusiast who has a lot of engagements, a very passionate man. He has been active in a number of different contexts throughout the last few years, and many of them simultaneously. He has been a social worker employed by the city of Gothenburg, runs his own business, and has been active as a volunteer in the sports movement. He enjoys and is stimulated by having many different roles and responsibilities. Not too long ago, he wrote the following note to me:

I feel that the more I have to do and the more different contexts and projects I involve myself in, the more evident it becomes how important having good structure is to maintaining a high quality in what I do. Structure helps me do many things at the same time, and to prioritize accurately among all the tasks every area in life contains. I believe that most things I do nowadays are completely in line with what my life is meant for, and as I told you previously, having good structure gives me more time to be who I truly am and want to be.

I can definitely relate to what Lasse is writing about, and to me, good structure is the prerequisite for living the life I lead.

How is the programme going? Feel free to write and tell me. You will reach me at super@stiernholm.com

ORGANIZE DAY 10:

KEEP LOOKING BACK

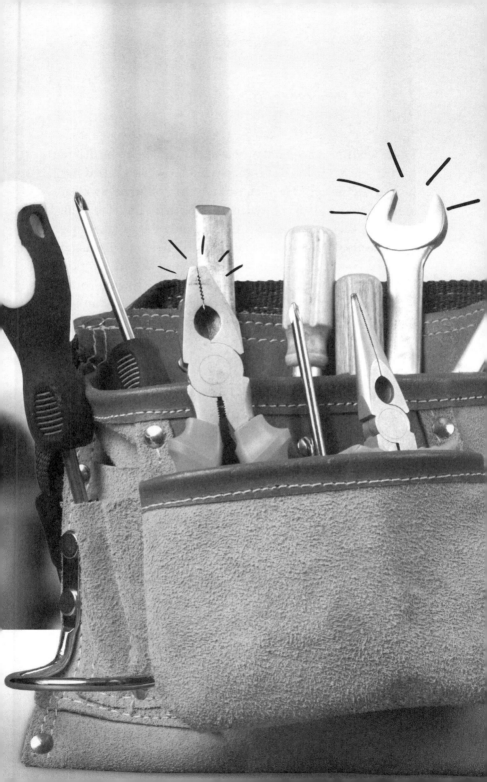

{ Proactivity gives you latitude. }

I have a business acquaintance who always used to be driving his car whenever I called him. No matter when I called him, he was "in the car." He often had to hurry off to help a client, and drive across half of Sweden only to attend a brief meeting, and then back home again. And not only did he often have to make these trips at the very last minute, but I frequently received emails from him late at night, as he was "working late to formulate an offer due for 9am tomorrow morning." Understandably, he was not very happy with this last-minute life, and he often both looked and felt pretty worn out.

I see this quite often in people I meet and help. They simply do not have enough foresight. Much more often than they would like, they realize, "What? Is this due tomorrow already?!" But you do not get good foresight automatically. If you are not currently working proactively, then we will have to create a routine that makes sure that you do: a routine that provides you with the ability to foresee and anticipate due dates and events.

TASK

First of all, decide on how and when you can take a breather to get an overview of all the structure tools discussed thus far, so that you can extend your foresight.

1. **Decide on how often you need to pause and get an overview.** Someone may feel that they need to do it every other week, someone else may feel that they need to do it every day, and another person may feel that they need to do

it once a week. Some people like doing this on Fridays so they can "close" the week and relax more during the weekend. Others prefer Mondays as it gives them a good start to the week. Or someone else may prefer to do it on Wednesdays because they then have half the week left to make up for anything they might have missed during Monday and Tuesday.

2. **Schedule a recurring meeting with yourself.** During these meetings you run through what has been done and what needs to be done. Set aside half an hour the first time, and make it longer next time if it turns out you need more time.

3. **Create a checklist of what you will then go through.** If you have a simple and easily available list, it is more likely that you will obtain the overview without hesitating about what the reminder "Get overview" in the calendar signifies. You can for instance create this checklist in a Word document, in the field for notes in the actual appointment inside your digital calendar, or on a neatly handwritten note pasted in an appropriate place. A few suggestions of what the checklist could contain are:
   - Update yourself on your long- and short-term goals. By doing so you will remind yourself of what truly matters (and what activities are useful to you when you are prioritizing your daily to-do tasks).
   - Skim through the to-do list. Check off anything that is already done. Add any new to-do tasks that come to your mind when viewing what is already on the list. Remove things you previously thought you would need to do, but that are no longer relevant or necessary.

- Go through your overview of major tasks and projects. Make sure you have defined the next step for each and every one of the projects. The next step should either be a to-do task that can be found on your to-do list, or something you are waiting for from someone else. Add any new projects you have initiated or been engaged in since your last update. Tick off and remove all completed projects.
- Take a look one month back in the calendar. If you recall something you have forgotten about, something which you may have promised to do for others as a result of attending meetings or having met certain people, then add them to your to-do list. This way, these to-do tasks are included in your daily prioritization as well.
- Take a look one month ahead in the calendar. Keep an eye out for any upcoming deadlines, and take a few moments to consider whether you need to prioritize a few tasks in the coming week so that you do not have to race against the clock on the last day before the deadline.

GAIN

If you get this kind of comprehensive overview as frequently as you need to, you will become more proactive in your work. This will result in you having fewer of those uncomfortable "Is that deadline next week already!" moments. Proactivity gives you latitude. If you have sufficient foresight, you can choose to do what you need to do related to a certain project when it suits you, rather than when you absolutely have to. Finishing things late or last minute is to tie your hands behind your back. It restricts you and strips you of the power to control what to do next as you do not really have a choice if you still want to finish what you promised before the deadline is up.

Browsing through your to-do list once in a while will give you more faith in the list as well. You will be able to park to-do tasks you do not want to do immediately and relax knowing that you will at least be reminded of it again soon. Hence it becomes much easier to let go of tasks for now and only concentrate on the ones that you are working on at that time. You will find that fewer things will be forgotten and involuntarily neglected if you skim through your to-do list on a regular basis and make sure that all projects always have the next step ready on the list as well.

REWARD

If you have scheduled the recurring meeting with yourself and created a checklist of what to do to get an overview, you are definitely worth a reward of your own choice.

THE FIRST TEN DAYS ARE OVER

Have you completed all of the first ten tasks? Well done! Did it take longer than ten days, even though you had the intention to keep to a faster pace? Not to worry. You have still reached this milestone and it means that you are well on your way to becoming more structured, and thus enjoying an easier and smoother life. I want to give you something extra for having done so well up till now. Your efforts are worth some additional acknowledgement.

Email me at super@stiernholm.com and tell me about how you are doing so far, and I will send you a treat. Remember to put "Super Structured" in the subject line. I am hoping to hear from you!

IN ORDER TO PRIORITIZE AND KNOW THAT YOU ARE DOING THE RIGHT THING AT THE RIGHT TIME, YOU NEED TO KNOW WHAT YOUR GOALS ARE.

"In the absence of clearly-defined goals, we become strangely loyal to performing daily trivia until ultimately we become enslaved by it."

Robert Heinlein (1907–1988)

FOCUS
DAY 11:

CLARIFY
YOUR
GOALS

A couple of years ago I helped structure a department of a business that had been created as a result of two organizations merging. The merger was quite recent and the reorganization involved had caused a lot of confusion and mess for the employees. Overall, all these changes had left the employees with much more to do than they could manage. They needed to understand how to prioritize in order to determine what tasks were more important so that they could complete these first. As there is never an objective answer as to what matters most in this world, they needed to lean on their goals and let these guide them when prioritizing. The goals of any business often consist of a detailed and concrete representation of the company's vision from a short-term perspective. The problem for this department was that the management of the new organization had not yet clearly defined the overall long-term nor the short-term goals for the new business. Hence the department experienced difficulties in defining their goals as they could not determine what the company's overall ambitions were. And because of this, it was virtually impossible for the employees to determine what their individual goals and responsibilities should be for the coming months. This meant that they were unable to distinguish which tasks were more important, what requests they should respond to first and simply what they should prioritize in their work. They had too much to do and did not have any tools to help them prioritize and hence obtain a manageable workload. It is important to know what your goals are in order to prioritize effectively and know that you're doing the right tasks at the right time.

TASK

Make it clear to yourself what goals you need or want to attain this year in the role you have in your business. Meaning:

1. Take a piece of paper and a pen, and write down the goals. They can be quantified goals or milestones (for instance that something needs to be completed by a certain date). If the goal is quantified or phrased as a key figure, make sure you write down what you are measuring and what value this measured unit should take for you to have achieved the goal. The more concrete, detailed, and in close correspondence with your daily activities the goal, the easier it is to determine which tasks matter more than others.

2. Think of something that allows you to visually see your goals every day so that you are reminded of them frequently. This could be:
   - a decision support system (it might even be in physical paper form, as the one that I have designed for myself and that you can find a template of at www.superstructured.com/decision-support)
   - a timeline with the milestones clearly marked out
   - an image depicting the goals that you use as a background on your computer desk-top
   - diagrams that you have printed out and stuck on the wall
   - a "progress bar" indicating how close you are to the milestone at the moment

- a gauge in some form where you indicate what value you are currently at, somewhat like a speedometer
- some other way in which you depict the goals visually and that brings a smile to your face every time you see it. (If you think of something brilliant, email me and tell me at super@stiernholm.com)

GAIN

By clarifying your goals, you will find it much easier to determine if you are doing the right things. When faced with having to prioritize tasks, your goals will help you to identify the to-do tasks that contribute more toward their achievement and hence identify which to-do task you should prioritize and do now. The result of all your efforts in the long run will also become more apparent, and you might now – to a greater extent than before – feel that your work is worthwhile, even on a rainy day when a potential client has rejected an offer you sent. If you are like me, you may find that having your goals in clear sight instead of hidden in a folder somewhere on the hard drive will help you to work with greater focus.

REWARD

When you have written down your goals and thought of at least one way to depict them visually, in a way that you are able to see them on a daily basis, reward yourself in that favourite way of yours. Enjoy the completion of yet another step in this process.

FOCUS DAY 12:

PRIORITISE YOUR TASKS

{ Refine your tasks based on the goals you are responsible for attaining. }

Last week I was at the lovely Aspenäs Manor House right outside of Gothenburg, where I gave a lecture on prioritization to a group of managers from a number of companies in the region. We were discussing the value of largely doing the things that contribute to the attainment of goals versus doing miscellaneous things that do not really accomplish anything long term. I asked the participants to think of tasks they do that do not contribute to reaching the goals they are responsible for. A woman who works with quality development in the chemical industry raised her hand and said: "I always say yes when asked to arrange the Christmas party and I definitely will not do so this year. The time I spend organizing the event certainly doesn't contribute to reaching the goals of our business."

I do not know the woman in question very well and have no perception of what her skills are as an event-organizer, but I suspect that there is a lot of work and effort involved in making the Christmas party happen every year. And I am also guessing that her core competences concern process development and poor quality costs rather than catering and sound systems. The party would probably be much more effectively organized by someone who does these things every day and who has refined their workflow and methods over time. And, I know the quality manager in question would have some weight lifted off her shoulders by delegating this project to someone else. She would then have more time and energy to improve the quality of their operations further, which will benefit her clients, her co-workers, and the company as a whole.

TASK

Sift and sort through your tasks and refine your to-do list in accordance to the business goals you are responsible for. Keep an eye out for to-do tasks you can eliminate or delegate so that you get more time for those tasks that truly matter.

1. You can download a refinement tool here: www.super-structured.com/refine

2. Go through your to-do list and have a closer look at the to-do tasks you have done in the past week.

3. Draw a table with three columns (or use the pre-drawn refinement tool downloaded in Step 1) that determines whether a particular to-do task contributes to your goals, namely the "Definitely" column, the "Probably" column and the "Surely not" column. Then decide and divide your tasks into these three columns.

4. Choose one of the to-do tasks in the "Surely not" column and decide to remove it completely. Your options are to never do the task again, delegate it to a colleague, or out-source it to someone outside of your business who will do it for you.

5. What might be the first step you could take to eliminate the task? It does not matter if it is a very small step. Define this first step as a to-do task and add it to your to-do list.

That is enough for today. Once you have taken the first step and checked it off the list, define the next step and add it to the to-do list as well (unless you do it straight away). Continue like this until you have finished the task completely. If you should feel like it, continue identifying more tasks to get rid of, go through the list again and enjoy getting more and more time for the tasks that truly contribute to achieving your goals.

The tasks you place in the "Definitely" column are the tasks that are most important to you. It's important to remember these when prioritizing between your tasks and projects in your everyday life and work. You can therefore consider the tasks in the "Probably" column to be semi-prioritized, on a more average level of priority.

GAIN
By doing this you will have more time to dedicate to the tasks that will help you to progress toward the goals you are responsible for in your business or company. You will accomplish more of what you want to achieve and only you know how important that is to you.

REWARD
If you find at least one task to place in the column "Surely not" and you define the first step of how to get rid of the task as a to-do task, you may reward yourself in the manner of your choosing.

FOCUS DAY 13: REFINE YOUR LIST

{   Create a checklist for emergencies.   }

My wife has ridden horses since she was a child. A few years ago we had the brilliant idea that I should learn to do this as well. We could then go to France and ride between picturesque castles in Bourgogne together. So, I started taking lessons at a riding school. It was a much more enjoyable experience than I could ever have imagined, and I particularly enjoyed riding and being around the larger horses. However, the whole project came to an unfortunate and abrupt end on a dark evening in January when my horse Martino was a little twitchier than usual. During an exercise in the riding school, when a drop of condensation fell from the rafters onto Martino's back, he jumped with fright and threw me off. When I stood up and brushed off the sawdust, I noticed that my fore-arm was hanging at my side at a very strange angle. It turned out that it was broken in a few places. A few bumpy and painful minutes after the fall, I was rushing to the emergency room, hyper-ventilating and in a state of shock. I was received by an emergency nurse who took care of me in the most professional manner. With a calm and soothing voice, she said: "David, I want you to have a seat right here. Breathe. You will be just fine. Here is some morphine."

On Day 12 you should have sifted through your tasks in a systematic and deliberate way. You should have sorted among the tasks while considering the goals that you want to reach. But, on particularly stressful and intense days when you may feel completely overwhelmed by the sheer number of tasks you have to finish, there is neither the time nor the mental space to fill out a form like Day 12's refinement tool quietly. No, on these occasions it's necessary to find a way to just get through the day and use the time available to do the right things.

When I have a really busy day, I sometimes find myself in "stress-limbo". I stare at the to-do list without finding and deciding on something to do next. I scroll up and down the email inbox without feeling like attending to anything in it. I am so overwhelmed by tasks demanding my attention that I freeze and I start my day with getting a cup of coffee and having a break to think about getting started – which then takes me even longer to get started. On such days, I need exactly what that emergency nurse gave me – simple, clear instructions I can follow one step at a time, and have faith that they will bring me back on track soon enough. When you are not stressed or under pressure, the instructions can appear ridiculously simple ("Sit down. Breathe."), but when you are in the middle of a stormy day, this simplicity is precisely what you need.

TASK

Create a short, clear checklist for times when you feel completely overwhelmed by everything you have to do, so that without even thinking about it you can get back on track and get started on the right things, even if it means that you manage to do fewer things than you might have wanted.

The checklist needs to contain a point that is about you getting an overview of everything you have to do, and some point where you choose what to do that day and what to do some other time. If you want to, have a look at mine. It goes something like this:

1. Take out the to-do list.

2. Disregard all the tasks that you do not have to do today and make sure that they vanish from view (that is, set a due date other than today or simply hide them).

3. Choose which three of the remaining tasks you will do first.

4. Do these three.

5. Start again from point 2 (because while you have been working, new to-do tasks might have been added to your list by colleagues, via phone, or through your email) and repeat the steps.

Save the list in such a way that you instantly can access it when you need it, without looking for it. It can be in either a physical or digital format. I keep my list in a simple text file on my computer, which I have made sure I can reach via a keyboard shortcut, as well as on one of the pages in the physical decision support system that I keep on my desk (and that I mentioned earlier).

GAIN

When you get to work and realize that it's going to be one of those days and you will not have the slightest chance to finish everything you need to do, take out the checklist and go through the steps. You will get started with doing tasks in the right order and according to your priorities. Notice how the stress and tension leaves you. You regain your motion instead of getting stuck in stress-limbo.

REWARD

When you have defined what steps your checklist will contain and saved it in an appropriate and easily accessible location, reward yourself in the way you previously determined you would.

FOCUS DAY 14:

ATTEND FEWER MEETINGS

{ ## Set a limit for the number of meetings you have in a day. }

There was a time in my professional life when I said yes to every meeting I was asked to attend, as long as there was space in my calendar on the suggested day and time. If I had a meeting scheduled for the time in question, I would suggest another day or time for the new one. It was therefore not uncommon for me to have up to four meetings a day, and often in different locations throughout the city. But, lo and behold, I also had tasks to complete which did not have anything to do with my meetings. As the majority of the hours of my working days were spent in meetings and travelling from one meeting to another, I had to resort to doing other tasks in the evenings and during the weekends. It was not a very pleasant or comfortable way of life. I wanted to spend my life doing more than just working, but there was not a lot of time left for anything else.

At the end of each day I always felt rather dazed because I would become deeply engaged in the conversations and encounters I'd had. Having four meetings a day definitely took its toll. If I had accepted fewer meetings in those days, I may have even been more alert during the final meeting of the day, but I rarely allowed myself this space and leeway. After a few days filled with meetings I could no longer recall what we actually said and decided on, as my memories of these meetings blended together more and more. Spending so much of my time in meetings made me feel stressed because I was unable to attend to other tasks. I knew that while I was in a meeting engaged in a conversation, I was receiving new emails but I was unable to attend to them. I knew that eventually, whenever I had a brief interlude between my overbooked days, I would have to plunge into my emails to address all these messages. I felt even more overwhelmed because I knew that my calendar would still be filled to the brim with meetings, and all the while I was still continuously receiving new emails.

Does any of this ring a bell? If so, then your life will be both more pleasant and efficient if you attend fewer meetings in a day. You will be able to focus more on what you are doing right now and feel less scattered. You will have more time and space to prepare for the next meeting. The quality of the meetings you do attend will undoubtedly be higher, and if you prioritize the right meetings (seen in relation to your goals) then you will reach the goals you are striving for faster and easier, but with less effort.

TASK

Decide on the maximum number of meetings you want attend each day. Make this into a rule for yourself: "I will attend a maximum of two meetings every day." If you want to remind yourself of your rule often, then schedule a recurring appointment (without setting a time for it) in your calendar. Name it something like "No more than two meetings today!" Most calendar programs will place bookings without a set time at the top of the day. This will be a useful reminder when you are asked to attend yet another meeting; as you check your availability on your calendar, you will undoubtedly be reminded of your new limit.

You will not have time for the same number of meetings as before, but this is a good thing. You are thereby forced to prioritize and mainly attend the meetings that really benefit you in your progress and in your business. You will say no to meetings that do not lead to anything (even if it seems nice to attend). At the same time you will make sure that the meetings you do attend really have substance and meaning. You will turn some meetings into phone conferences or conduct the discussions via email. In many cases you'll find this to be more effective as you will only address the matters needing immediate attention and not easily deviate off on tangents or socialize as you would otherwise.

GAIN

If you decrease the number of meetings you have during a workday, you will be more present and attentive during the meetings you do attend. By attending just one less hour-long meeting at least every other day, you will save 125 hours per year. You will be less stressed and able to work with focus on the tasks that contribute to the attainment of your goals. It totals up to almost three work-weeks. And if the meetings that you choose not to attend are the ones that don't really have an agenda or a true purpose, and where you would have felt as if you had been "taken hostage" as your department's representative, then you have just made your life considerably better.

REWARD

If you decide on a limit for the maximum number of meetings you attend in a day and think of a clever way to remind yourself of the rule as you are about to check your availability for yet another get-together, then reward yourself plentifully in that way you like so much. You are definitely worth it. You have taken a very effective step toward having more focused and purposeful workdays.

FOCUS DAY 15:

TAKE A BUFFER DAY

{ If we acknowledge the progress we make,
no matter how small it may seem,
we will perceive life in a brighter light. }

How are you doing so far? Are you keeping the pace you wanted to begin with? Are you moving swiftly and steadily toward having excellent structure? I am sure you have made progress somehow, at least in something. I am giving you another buffer day today with which you may do as you please. If you have fallen behind this is a great time to catch up. If not, then look back at what you have done thus far and notice the things you have already changed and now take for granted.

Teresa Amabile, Professor of Business Administration at Harvard Business School, has shown in her research that the small "victories" we experience on a daily basis significantly influence what she refers to as our "inner work life". By acknowledging progress, no matter how small it may seem, you will perceive life in a brighter light, feel better, and become more motivated. She suggests that through registering and visualizing progress somehow, you can make it clear to yourself that you have actually made progress.

Think of a way to clearly show yourself that you are moving forward through this structure improvement programme. Will you draw a little mark on the whiteboard for every small victory? Will you check another box? Add another cotton pulp ball to a see-through pipe? Think of a way that motivates you. There is no "right" or "wrong" way of doing this, just do what you feel would motivate you. Through the years, I have nailed various "proofs of success" to my wall, added values in an iPhone app and drawn diagrams, so there are all kinds of ways to illustrate the results of your efforts.

FOCUS
DAY 16:

REDUCE YOUR
DISTRACTIONS

{ Go from chaos to quiet whenever you need to. }

The other day I gave a lecture in the newly renovated premises of a large Swedish corporation. There was a high ceiling, the furniture was exquisite and ... they had open-plan offices. I asked my host how she gets on with working as a salesperson in such an open environment. She replied: "It has been difficult to get used to. Especially for those of us that have to make many calls a day, and who previously had our own offices where we could close the door when we wanted some peace and quiet. It is easier to get distracted now. Right when you are in the middle of something, a colleague's phone rings and as he has a popular song as his ringtone, you think 'Oh, that's that song...', and then you're suddenly distracted and completely off track."

It was interesting to hear her describe her situation as I perceive this type of office environment in the same way. A thought occurred to me: is there really anyone who enjoys working in an open-plan office? I asked around in my network and received some unexpected answers. About three quarters of the people I spoke to felt that open-plan made their work more difficult as they were easily distracted by all the things going on around them. But, the other quarter experienced the contrary – they felt inspired and stimulated by what others perceived as disturbing distractions and noise. They described how they need to have a bit of movement around them to get up to speed themselves. They were inspired and got ideas when they overheard colleagues talking a few paces away. They were stimulated by the feeling of togetherness and by being able to ask for the opinions of colleagues sitting nearby.

However, for the majority of the people I meet through my work, distractions generally make them less effective than they would be if they could work undisturbed. It is also a question of context: sometimes we have tasks that need to be done right now, and that requires our full attention. When this is the case, we really need to be able to focus.

The architect and researcher Christina Bodin Danielsson is active within Brunnberg & Forshed Architects as well as at the Stress Research Institute at Stockholm University. Bodin Danielsson studied the types of offices that people enjoy and feel good working in, and the types of environments that make work more satisfying, in her dissertation for the Kungliga Tekniska Hogskolan [Royal Institute of Technology] in 2010. Her results were very interesting. She found that cellular offices (meaning, separate offices) and flex offices (no permanently assigned seats, but plenty of secluded spaces to withdraw into and be alone in) were the most popular ones and the ones that benefited our well-being the most. The results showed further that for the medium- and small-sized office landscapes (with assigned seats), the risk for ill health and poor well-being was on the other hand significantly higher. Bodin Danielsson suggests that this is because we can influence our situation and surroundings the most in cellular offices and flex office spaces. If we want peace and quiet, we can achieve it instantly by closing our door or seating ourselves in a quiet room. In an open landscape, we have no control of the circumstances and have to deal with the noise.

I recently met Linda Tufvasson, the Creative Director at Struktur, a company that improves working environments in businesses and organizations. She told me that the flex office model in the shape of activity-based workplaces is becoming increasingly popular and that it is evolving into an open landscape divided into sections that are adapted for different tasks or activities. So, each section represents a different type of environment within the same space. There are zones designed specifically to enable concentration, communication zones, collaboration zones, and quiet zones. If you just want to quickly check your email before going into the next meeting, you can take a seat in the touchdown zone, which is designed to be a place where you just sit down temporarily – this is achieved by providing furniture that is not very comfortable, so the user will not be encouraged to remain for longer than 20 minutes. Some tasks are great for doing in the coffee shop resembling "coffice" section of the landscape, and if you are constantly on the move and on the phone, you can step into one of the phone booths standing along the wall to get a few moments peace and quiet when making a call. The important improvement made by this model is that the office staff know and can choose where and how to work, even though they are still in an open landscape.

If you need some peace and quiet from time to time to really focus on a particular task, there are thankfully several things you can do, even if you cannot change your entire office environment in a trice. If you make it clear to yourself right now what you could do to improve your situation, then you will quickly go from chaos to quiet whenever you need to.

TASK

Think of three ways you could enable yourself to work undisturbed and focused. These could for instance be:

- Closing the door. It's great to be available to discuss things with colleagues. But that is only true if interruptions aren't met with subdued frustrations which can be the case if the person being disturbed actually wants to be left alone.

- Turning off your phone. If you do not wish to be available for calls, the easiest way to ensure you do not receive any is to turn off the phone. Pretty straightforward, don't you think?

- Closing down any social media you tend to get distracted by. Staying in touch with customers and colleagues as well as being updated on industry news is essential, but maybe not entirely necessary this very moment, when you really need to focus?

- Shut down the company chat client if you are using one. Short messaging is often an efficient alternative to email, but if you have prioritized deliberately with your goals in mind and found out what to-do task is the right thing to work on right now, do you really want to be distracted by this and that, that probably is less urgent and less important?

- Put on your headphones and listen to some music. Or, you could listen to "brown noise", a synthetically produced noise that, among other things, is used to relieve tinnitus.

- Go into a quiet room. If you are lucky, your office has quiet rooms for you to use when you need to work in silence.

- Book a conference room. If it feels like booking an entire room to yourself is overdoing it, bring a few colleagues along that also need to concentrate, and you can share the silence while working. If it works in quiet reading rooms at the library, it will work in your office as well.

- Work from home. Your colleagues are far away at the office and you are only virtually present and visible to them if you choose to be.

- Work at your favourite café where the environment is a balance between inspiring chaos and soothing murmur.

- Get a room at a hotel. You can work completely undisturbed and still have full service in terms of meals and other comforts.

- Log out from your email account. If you are naturally curious (like me) and rarely resist the temptation to constantly check for new messages, you will be able to focus a lot more by simply logging out from your account or shutting down the email program.

- Close down your internet connection. If you are continually doing miscellaneous things online when you should be getting on with getting something else done, make sure you stay away by re-sorting to slightly more drastic measures. Pull the plug, or use a program such as Freedom (freedom.to) where you indicate for how long you wish to stay away from the web. Once you have clicked "OK", you have to restart your computer if you want to go online again before the time-limit is up.

- Write in a program free from distractions. There are a handful of software and programs that allow you to write text without getting distracted by spell-check, formatting, buttons, menus, and settings. Instead of getting confused by all these options, you can focus fully on what you have to write. My favourite program is OmmWriter (www.ommwriter.com) and there are several commonly used word processing programs that have view modes which are free from many of their somewhat distracting functions and menus.

REWARD

If you have thought of three ways to work undisturbed and undistracted, then reward yourself in the way you chose. If in addition to this you have done something concrete to make these three solutions more accessible to you, then you deserve an extra pat on the back. You might for instance have explained to your colleagues that you are not available for questions when you have your headphones on or decided where you will escape to when you really need to be alone.

Well done! You have just made sure that you will be distracted less during your workdays.

FOCUS DAY 17:

SCHEDULE SOME SOLO TIME

{ If you create a better balance between the time spent in meetings and time spent working alone, you will work less overtime. }

I once met the CEO of a medium-sized Swedish company who told me: "I would really love to be able to close my door to work undisturbed once in a while." Many people I meet suffer from this ailment of availability. We confuse the well-intentioned idea that "my door is always open" with that we always have to be available for colleagues and clients. Of course there are those whose work is all about answering questions and being available for others, but most people also have tasks to do on their own. It is important to allow the time needed for these tasks as well.

By getting better at making the necessary time available for your own tasks, you will find that you do not have to spend weekends and evenings doing them (at times when your colleagues have left for the day and no one is there to disturb you or ask you to attend a meeting).

TASK
Do this:

1. Think about how much time you need every week for working uninterrupted on your own, without really interacting with colleagues. One way to estimate the time needed is to look through your to-do list and estimate the amount of time every such task will take (one week at a time).

2. Look through your calendar and try to think of when it's usually a quiet time for you during the week, and when you can get some alone-time effortlessly.

3. Now decide on one, or several set times every week when you will work alone and undisturbed. It can be as little as half an hour, a few hours or even a whole day that you reserve for working alone in your office without any meetings or other major interruptions.

4. Well done. Now you have made up your mind, all you need to do is to remember this decision and follow it through. Reserve the alone-time you feel that you need in your calendar. You can for instance create a parallel calendar in a different colour that can be turned on or off, and where you see what times you would prefer to work alone. This becomes a template to have a look at when scheduling things in your ordinary calendar, rather than a second calendar to keep track of. Or, add the times you feel you need to work alone in your calendar and name them "Free time", highlight these by using a different colour than used for your ordinary appointments. This way it becomes easier to stay clear of meetings during these times, and you will not fill up the calendar without including your much needed alone-time.

If you cannot dedicate as much time as you would like to working undisturbed, there are a few other things you can do. You can sift out some of the to-do tasks categorized as "on my own" so that you end up with fewer of these, or you can decline more requests to attend meetings. If all the meetings you need to attend and all the other tasks you have to do, do not fit within reasonable working hours, you have basically too much to do and need to stop doing certain things, delegate more, or outsource more tasks so that you have energy for the most important things you need to do.

GAIN

If you can create a better balance between the time spent in meetings and the time you need to work alone on tasks, you will no longer need to work overtime as often as before. As you probably do not tend to schedule meetings during the evenings, you will be forced to prioritize your meetings and tasks more. However, if you enjoy working during evenings, then schedule your alone-time for evenings instead of cramming them into free minutes between meetings, which will probably only make you more stressed and frustrated.

REWARD

Reward yourself abundantly if you manage to figure out how much time you need for working undisturbed during an average week. Even if this is only an educated guess, reserve the time that you need in your calendar so that your decision to respect your own time-frames becomes concrete and easy to heed.

FOCUS DAY 18:

MAKE MEETINGS MORE EFFICIENT

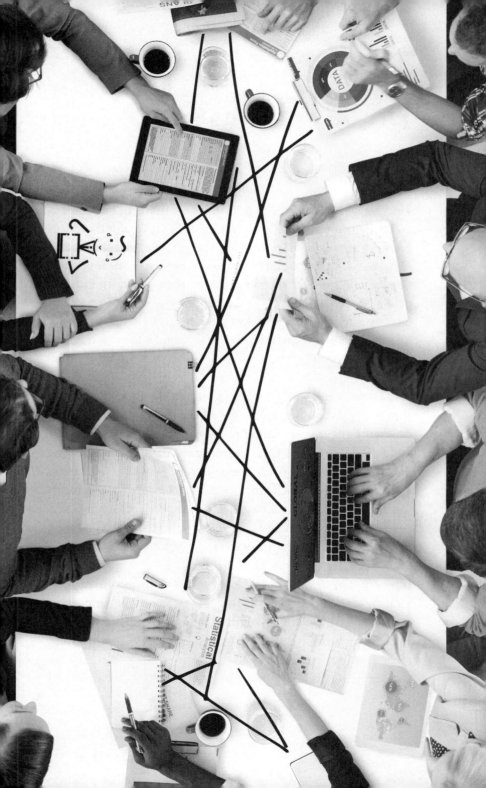

{ Say no to meetings without an agenda. }

When was the last time you were in a meeting? I am guessing it was not too long ago. Perhaps you just walked out of one. Thus far we have discussed limiting the number of meetings to create the time needed to attend to other tasks. But there will be times where we need to meet with people, and it is useful to make use of available techniques to optimize our meetings. Good techniques for meetings can be regarded as an art, and deserve a whole book on the topic. But as we spend so much of our time in meetings, it makes sense for us to dedicate at least one day to doing something concrete to make the meetings we do attend more efficient.

A few years ago I worked with a group of experts who felt that they really did not have time for all the things they needed to do during an ordinary workday. We got talking about meetings and I asked them how their meetings normally proceed. Some of them answered: "Well, when we say 'let's have a meeting about it', we always schedule at least two hours for the meeting and make sure we have time for a cup of coffee and some cake as well." I might add that their daily schedule contained at least one or two, and sometimes more, of these meetings.

If we are approaching meetings from a structure point of view, and are concerned with having time for all the important tasks we need to do, the length of an average meeting is definitely something we should strive to shorten. If we feel that most meetings are longer than they need to be (even if they are shorter than two hours), then let us cut the time we spend on them in half, at least for a few weeks, and then evaluate them. While working on this book I have asked a number of people what their best tricks are for making their meetings more efficient. The best responses I got were:

- Set an agenda for the meeting, even if it is informal. Think through the structure of the meeting in advance, what decisions you want to make and the next steps that you want the participants to agree on.

- Say no to meetings without an agenda.

- Set a timeframe for the agenda. Estimate the amount of time every question and issue will take, and write it out on the agenda.

- Create a template for the agenda of recurring meetings so that you do not have to start from scratch every week.

- Create a routine for meetings which outlines how far ahead of the meeting, where, and in what format you will publish the agenda and any additional materials.

- For every point on the agenda, clarify what type of item it is. A few suggestions are: Information, Decision, and Discussion.

- Turn off mobile phones. I am of the radical opinion that if you are not able to or you do not want to answer phone calls, then the phone should be switched off completely. If you are obligated to keep it switched on – if, for instance, you are the head of security at a nuclear power plant – then you should of course leave it on.

- Schedule meetings that tend to become lengthy for an hour, or 90 minutes, before lunchtime. The participants will be keen to get the meeting done so they can get their lunch.

- Schedule several internal meetings after one another (and preferably in the same room). This way it becomes less likely that they continue past the set ending-time.

- If you meet clients with whom you have a well-established and easy-going relationship, then tell them how much their first ten minutes of chit-chat actually costs them, but in a jovial and fun way.

- Have your meetings during the first half of the day, if that is when you feel the most alert.

- Appoint someone as the facilitator or moderator of your meetings, if you do not already have one.

- Make sure to come prepared. If you make it a habit of skimming though your calendar once every week, then you will be reminded of any upcoming meetings. This makes it easier to read or prepare materials well ahead of the meeting.

TASK

1. Choose one or a few things you will begin to implement in your meetings from now on. It could be one of the suggestions mentioned above, or some other idea you have to improve your meetings.

2. Pick just one of the improvements to begin with.

3. Decide what meeting you will try your new strategy on for the first time. Will you try it during the management meeting next month? Will it be the next client meeting you schedule? Or is it the Monday meeting with the staff?

4. Now do whatever you need to do to prepare the first trial of your new approach.

GAIN

One of my clients, a human resources manager in a medium-sized organization, started making meeting notes in a more structured way than she used to. She made sure to clearly separate the next steps that were decided on during the meetings from other meeting notes. This simple step made it easier for her to define her to-do tasks and get going much faster on these next steps. After a month, she told me that she had increased the number of decisions she makes by 40%, which she believed was because of her improved structure and clear method of making it easier to progress.

When it comes to having more efficient meetings, we can achieve significant results by small means. If you can cut the time you spend in meetings by half, you will free up an enormous amount of time for doing other tasks. Keep in mind that you still need to manage addressing all that needs your attention during the meetings – cutting them shorter but at the cost of reducing the quality of your work is never worth it and does more damage than good.

REWARD

If you have chosen or thought of at least one improvement you want to make, tested it out, and then evaluated its effect, then reward yourself in the way you previously determined.

FOCUS DAY 19:

REFINE YOUR PRIORITIES

{ Abstain! }

"Now I can see what we are doing!", the development manager at an IT company exclaimed during a workshop I held for the management group. He went on: "We keep initiating new projects but after a while we have too much to do, so our management group meets and discusses which projects to prioritize. We decide on the order of priority, but then we continue working on all the projects like before anyway, and just put in a little extra effort into the three projects we agreed to focus on. So, instead of reducing our workload, we are actually increasing it!"

Prioritizing is all about abstaining. This means making an active decision not to do certain things. In order to create more time for our more important tasks, we need to choose not to do certain other tasks, or at least temporarily abandon them. The projects we have to let go of can be either paused or delegated to someone else. Are they urgent? Well, perhaps they should be prioritized then, if they also are important. Maybe you do not have time for them? Then you do not have enough people working on the things you want to get done in your company and instead need to outsource. You do not have the resources? Good. Then you need to prioritize. Choose the tasks and projects that you need to abstain from working on.

TASK

If you realize that you have projects on your project overview that you do not actually have time for, then move them to some kind of "project parking lot" and attend to them when you have more time and energy. Just as you are not physically able to work on an infinite number of to-do tasks, you cannot be involved in too many projects at the same time.

1. Create a place or list in conjunction with your project overview (preferably in the same format or program) to park the projects you will put on hold for now, until the right moment comes to work on them again.

2. Check in with your boss, your colleagues, your management group, and anyone else who is involved in the projects you are putting on hold and hence are affected by you doing so.

3. Set a date for a "project audition", meaning when you take out the "project parking lot", and go through the projects parked on it to see if any of these need to be revived and resumed.

4. Add a to-do task to your to-do list that describes what you need to do to make this "audition" happen. You might, "Go through the project parking lot and consider if any of the projects parked there qualify to become active once again" or "Add an item to the agenda for the next management group meeting regarding evaluating possible projects to reactivate". If you have not defined to yourself how to reactivate parked projects, chances are that you may forget that they exist and then not dare to put any others aside in the future.

GAIN

If you prioritize more, you will have more time to do the tasks that are truly important faster and with higher quality. You will experience having the time you need to be thorough and deliver what matches your high standards and level of ambition. You will finish fewer things at the last minute and not have a perpetually bad conscience for not performing at the top of your game.

REWARD

If you have created a project parking lot that is stable and where you can easily park projects, then reward yourself in that favourite way of yours. Also reward yourself if you have defined a foolproof way to ensure that the projects are not forgotten and end up in the parking lot indefinitely.

FOCUS DAY 20:

ESTABLISH AN ORGANISED TIMELINE

{ Doing the right thing
at the right time. }

Yesterday afternoon I visited a multinational company that I am hoping will become one of my new clients. Toward the end of the meeting I promised to email prices and more detailed presentations and descriptions of the services we discussed. We agreed that we would be in touch in a few weeks, and I left. When I got to the office today I had planned to write a few chapters of this book first thing in the morning, but I wanted to send that email first. I realized that before doing so I had to put together an additional page presenting my services on the Stiernholm Consulting website, and suddenly a whole hour had passed before I got around to writing. A long-term, highly important task (writing my book) had to wait so that I could send that urgent email.

But, to be honest, how urgent was it really? Today is the Thursday before Easter, when a lot of people in Sweden usually stay at home, and I am not even sure the woman at the large company was at work today. And if she is working, she might have a whole pile of tasks to complete before Easter, so my email would be the last thing she would attend do, if she even got around to it today. I might just have prioritized the recent and seemingly urgent task before the long-term and important one for nothing. So in the hour I spent creating the material, I could probably have written this whole chapter.

It is important for me (and I am guessing for you as well) to do what I want done as easily as possible, and one way of ensuring this is to do the right thing at the right time. The more aware we are of when something needs to be completed, the easier it becomes to prioritize accurately. If everything that lands on our desks needs to "be done as soon as possible", we have no other option than throwing ourselves at whatever it might be and doing it as quickly as possible, even though we have to stress and hurry to finish it. But if we know that we have plenty of time to finish, we will be free to choose the task we feel like doing right now. And by doing so, we will finish more tasks with considerably greater ease.

DON'T DO WHAT I DID YESTERDAY

If you are about to promise someone something, ask when they need it. Yes, I know, it might seem obvious. Yet, I still did not ask this question yesterday. Apparently doing so was not a habit yet. But it will be from now on.

TASK

When someone asks you to do something today, ask them when they need it. Make sure you leave the conversation with a clear deadline so that it becomes easier to prioritize among all your tasks. In order to establish the habit of always asking and making sure you have a clear due date for assignments, think of a simple reward you will give yourself every time you remember to ask. Ask as often as you can remember, and reward yourself every time.

GAIN

If you get an idea of what expectation people have regarding when they want whatever it is that they have requested, you will get a lot more of the "important, but not urgent" tasks done. These are the tasks which you would otherwise postpone because of lack of time. And as it so happens, these tasks are often the ones that make your business progress and grow. If these types of tasks are done sooner, your whole company will develop faster and more steadily in the direction you are striving toward, as even the biggest changes happen in small steps.

REWARD

If you asked someone when they need what they asked you to do and you agreed upon when the thing is due, reward yourself in the way you chose at the beginning of this structure improvement programme.

EASE YOUR BURDENS.

AUTOMATE DAY 21:

PREDICT THE PREDICTABLE

You have now got as far as the third phase on your path to becoming super-structured. You have organized your work and increased your capacity to focus. It is now time to further ease your burdens. By automating more tasks and processes at work, you will find that you need to exert less effort in getting them done.

In this digital age, the number of apps and services that help us automate small and large tasks is increasing rapidly and any recommendations I would give here would soon be outdated. If you want my tips on the best digital tools for everyday work automation right now, turn to the list I keep updated at www.superstructured.com/automate.

Instead, let us in this phase focus on what automations we can create that do not depend on a particular digital tool.

Automating as much as possible what we need to get done really simplifies our workdays. This is particularly true for when you need to remember to do something. Often, you'll find that you do certain tasks on a regular basis, but perhaps not often enough to make them a habit and remember how the task is done.

At the moment I have a client who travels to the other side of the country to meet with his boss for a progress report on the same date every month. About a week before the meeting he needs to book tickets and a few days before departure he needs to compile a simple report as well as prepare a presentation. Until not too long ago, more often than not, he would remember that he had to write the report the night before it was due and, as he had forgotten to book a flight, he had to throw himself in his car and drive in the middle of the night in order to arrive at the meeting on time.

By automatically getting reminded of predictable tasks you will no longer have to remember them, but you will be sure that "someone" will remind you to do the task on its due date. My client now allows his to-do tool to remind him when it is time to book a flight and compile the report every month.

TASK

1. Make a list of all the recurring to-do tasks you can think of on a piece of paper or in a document. If you find it helpful, place them under headlines such as: "Every day", "Every week", "Every month", "Every quarter", "Every year" and so on. Use just as much detail and phrase them concretely, as you would when you formulate your to-do tasks.

2. If you find it difficult to think of to-do tasks, ask yourself if on a regular basis you do anything concerned with: finance, statistics, staff, reporting, coordinating with someone, registration, prices, contracts, working environment, 5S, market activities, and clients.

3. Add these tasks as recurring to-do tasks in the tool you use to manage your to-do tasks. If you have several to-do tasks that you need to be reminded of, I recommend that you choose to use a digital tool. Then you will not have to do anything in addition to adding the to-do task in order to remember it; the tool will remember everything for you. You simply indicate how often you wish to be reminded and can relax because the tool will let you know when it is time to do it. If you still prefer working with pen and paper, create a list for every time-period and make it into a habit to look at the lists every day to see if the due date of any scheduled event is approaching.

4. Done!

GAIN

By allowing the tool you have chosen for your to-do list to keep track of all your recurring tasks, you will not have to remember to write them down over and over again. Not only will you not have to do the work (and hence save time), but you can also rest assured that you will not forget to add the tasks next month as it now happens automatically.

REWARD

If you have written down all recurring tasks you can think of and entered them into your tool, reward yourself in the way you previously said you would. Enjoy having automated some of your to-do tasks in a very simple way.

AUTOMATE DAY 22:
CONSIDER YOUR APPROACH

"If you don't have time to do it right, when will you have time to do it over?"

{ Enjoy the changes you
have accomplished. }

Today you get another buffer day! Use it to catch up if you have fallen behind. If you are on track with the programme, then just take the day to enjoy the changes and progress you have made. And if you have time, allow me to share one of the quotes that inspire me the most right now:

"If you don't have time to do it right, when will you have time to do it over?"

I read this quote by John Wooden, an American basketball coach at UCLA, a few weeks ago and it really struck a chord with me. Due to a combination of an eagerness to continuously progress and a tad of indolence, I have a persistent tendency to hasten on to the next task, and then the next, instead of being fully present and concentrated on what I am currently doing. Often the result is that I procrastinate on the final steps and the actual completion of tasks until later. And this in turn only makes me feel as if I have much more to do, as I keep adding to my list of things to finish, and I eventually end up feeling exhausted and stressed.

But Wooden's reflection really made me stop and think about this tendency and pattern. I wrote the quote on a sheet of paper and hung it from the wire I have fastened across my office, where I hang inspirational images. Since I did this, I have been greeted by these wise words every time I step into my office, and believe it or not, the words must have slowly permeated my subconscious because I actually notice a distinct difference in how I now act in terms of completing tasks. To a significantly greater extent than before, I now take the time to finish what I start, and do not let a task go until I am completely satisfied. In fact, I have even caught myself doing more things well ahead of when they are due than I used to. I feel as if I now have some sort of argument to use against myself and my tendency to jump between tasks. This has helped me to become more thorough and follow tasks through to completion instead of starting (but not always finishing) as many tasks as possible.

Perhaps it is a little early to determine what long-term effects this tweak of my behaviour will have on my life, but the results so far are definitely a good start.

If you want to indoctrinate yourself with a positive message that you can embrace and incorporate into your life, where would you put it (so that you see it often) and in what format?

AUTOMATE DAY 23:

HELP YOURSELF WITH A CHECKLIST

{ When it comes to automating things that need to run smoothly in our lives, the checklist is the tool that will help us the most. }

I gave a talk to a unit at a large public organization last week. During a break I spoke with one of the administrators who told me that they had a situation a while back where all of the administrators were handling their cases differently. They were all doing what they were supposed to, but their ways of documenting what they had done varied considerably. It was very difficult for an administrator to answer questions regarding another colleague's cases as they did not understand the structure of their colleague's notes and materials. With a legitimate pride in her voice the administrator told me that they had recently done something about this problem, and agreed on how the process should run, what it should contain, and how they would document their work. And by doing so, they had developed a checklist containing all the steps of the process. They now attach a copy of the checklist (digitally) to every new case that accompanies it throughout the whole process, from start to finish. The administrator checks each of the steps off the list gradually, and makes notes in the designated place and in the correct format.

So in what way has this made things easier for them? Well, as everyone is working according to the same method, things run more smoothly as no one has to remember or reinvent what next steps to take. And if you are asked something about a certain case, any one of the administrators can retrieve the right information with ease, regardless of who had been responsible for the case. The clients get answers to their queries faster and the administrators' work has become easier. Everyone is enjoying the fruits of this improvement.

When it comes to automating things that need to run smoothly in our lives, the checklist is a tool that will help us immensely. And yet, it is not used as much as it should be. For most of us, the tasks we do on a daily basis are tasks we have either done before, or that resemble things we have previously done. If we create a checklist for these tasks, we will have to exert less effort remembering steps of the process and how to do them. Things get done faster, it becomes easier to do them, and we can spend more time and energy on the tasks that need our full concentration and attention.

For a while, I had an assignment that required me to do the same task once a month. The task had 36 steps and it was crucial that I did them in the right order. The checklist outlining the 36 steps helped me to make sure I never got lost in the process and that I always knew exactly where I was. It reminded me of how to do everything and made sure I did not miss a step. I could turn on some music, open the checklist, and just do the task without really making an effort. As I was clear on what to do and how to do it, I was more relaxed and never procrastinated about the task, which I otherwise probably would have with a more ambiguous process. Besides, making a checklist is incredibly simple.

You will have time to do one today, even if you have a lot on your plate.

TASK

1. Take a moment to think about what you have to do today (or have a look at your to-do list).

2. Pick a task from the things you are doing today that you will need to do again some other time.

3. When it is time to do the task, equip yourself with a blank sheet of paper or create a new document in a word processing program.

4. As you go about the task, write down what you do, step by step. Copy and paste any shortcuts to files and links if it helps you find the right material or websites the next time you are going to do the task. Write down any codes and abbreviations you use, but be careful with passwords. The more detailed you are, the longer it will take to create the checklist, but the easier your work will become the next time you are going to do the same task. It is a matter of how much time and effort you are ready to invest now, and how big you want the return to be.

5. When will you do the task next time? Think of a foolproof way to remember to use the checklist the next time you are doing this task. You could for instance refer to the checklist in the description of the to-do task.

6. If you think of more tasks that would be easier with a checklist, add new to-do tasks to your list along the lines of: "Write a checklist for [the task in question]".

Now, wasn't that easy? It is wonderful that something so simple can and will help you so much, and make things so much easier.

GAIN

If you make checklists for recurring tasks, you will complete them faster and with higher quality. If you should get interrupted while working on them, you just mark out where you are in the checklist and resume your work with ease once you are back at your desk again. You will never have to start all over because you missed a step early on in the process, and if there are several people who are doing the same tasks, it will be much easier to stick to the process you agreed on by using checklists.

REWARD

If you create a checklist for one of your tasks today and refine it at least in some respect (for instance by clarifying something, changing the order in which you do the steps, adding useful information or something else that makes the process easier), then reward yourself in the way you previously determined you would.

AUTOMATE DAY 24:

KEEP YOUR CHECKLIST CONVENIENT

{ Describing routines is one thing, using them in your everyday life another. }

Once upon a time, there was a quality system. With a lot of effort and great difficulty, the employees of the company had defined and described their processes and routines under the supervising eye of an enthusiastic project manager. It was tedious work, and when they were finally done, they had assembled process descriptions, checklists, and other quality documents that were systematically organized and stored in the intranet so that everyone had access to them. The intention was that they should then be able to look up how various processes and routines were to be done so that the quality of their common work was not only maintained, but enhanced as well. But as time went by, fewer of the employees made use of the quality system or visited the URL where their documentation was published. What initially gave a comprehensive overview of the company's operations, soon felt out of date.

Describing and documenting routines is one thing, but actually using and implementing them in your everyday work and life is something else. If you are to reap the benefits of the checklists you have created (and will create in the future), you need to store them somewhere where they are easily accessible to you.

TASK

1. Decide on where and how you will store your checklists. Consider:
   - Will they be digital or physical?
   - Will they be gathered in one location, or should they be located together with the material used when doing the task they describe?
   - If they are digital, how are you going to name the files consistently so that you find them easily when searching for them?
   - Will you be the only one using them or will you share them with colleagues as well?

2. When you have answered these questions, do what you need to do to create this location. Create the folder, order the manuscript holder you want on your desk, add an item to the agenda of next department meeting where you present the ideas you have for your new working method, or do something else.

GAIN

If you store the checklists in a way that they are truly accessible and you actually use them frequently, you will enjoy the benefits of not having to reinvent the processes every time you perform certain tasks. But if you should hide them away somewhere where you eventually will not even remember putting them, you miss the point and miss out on the assistance they could have provided you with. It is as simple as that.

REWARD

If you create a storage place for your checklists and add your first list to it, then reward yourself as usual. Well done!

AUTOMATE DAY 25:

GET OFF TO A GOOD START

{ ## What do you need to do to get a perfect start to your workday? }

Jacob Folkesson was working hard in front of the computer. And he was enjoying it. He had really gotten into that wonderful feeling of "flow" and everything felt so easy. He devoted himself to the tasks ahead and checked them off one by one as he completed them. It went easier and faster than he had thought it would. Six months ago his situation was completely different. He was constantly stressed, tense, and distracted. New emails kept dropping into his inbox, and he was jumping from one task to another to put out fires. When he got to the office in the mornings, he opened his laptop and worked frenetically the whole day, and sometimes late into the night as well. And yet he never seemed to finish. There was always something more that needed doing. Every Friday night he left the office utterly exhausted and with a gnawing anxiety that he had missed something.

But then something happened! One late Tuesday afternoon he realized that he had spent his entire day doing whatever popped up instead of writing that offer he had promised a client to send the same day. He realized that even though he had seen himself as a capable and vigorous person, he still did not seem to have control over his time. New things requiring his attention kept showing up to interrupt and divert him, but he had had enough. From now on he would work more consciously, deliberately, and systematically. He thought to himself: "If I am going to change how I go about my days, I have to start by doing things differently in the morning."

And what could he do in the morning to ensure that he got a better grasp of the rest of the day? Well, he used to get brilliant ideas on the way to work and by the time he arrived, he would be immersed in the new idea and eagerly start working on them first thing as he sat down by his desk. After working with inspiration and zest for a while, he accidentally opened the calendar and realized to his horror that he was expected in a meeting on the other side of town in just a few minutes.

So, if Jacob began his day by quickly checking the calendar to remind himself of what meetings and appointments he had to remember throughout the day, this would not happen again. But, he thought, it does not have to be a meeting. It might be a task that is particularly urgent, such as something he needs to send off before 9am. So, he also decided to skim through his to-do list right after checking his calendar as he arrived in the morning to see if there were any tasks he needed to prioritize and do straight away. Now his day would start by doing two things that could prevent stress and disasters.

After a few days, Jacob noticed that he tended to forget checking his to-do list. He kept getting stuck in his email instead. That was where the action was at. "But why should I focus so much on my emails anyway? Who says that the emails that I receive are the tasks I should be prioritizing, just because they are emails? They could be about absolutely anything, not just important things," he thought. The mornings after he also started another habit of going through recently received emails and creating to-do tasks for those he did not reply to immediately, hence enabling himself to accurately prioritize among all his tasks and emails.

In the following weeks, this routine grew to encompass more and more elements of his work, and he eventually used most of his time at work choosing what to do consciously. Jacob decided to establish another routine to process the physical documents he was given in the same way as the digital emails. For every unit of paper or material he was given, he made a decision if he was going to do something with or about it straight away (a to-do task), if he needed to save it, or if he could throw it away. He managed to get rid of the pile of papers that had amassed on his desk until there was no longer a pile.

Jacob also noticed that he was not accurately estimating the times when he would be able to do things. This frequently resulted in the day's to-do list being longer than he had time to finish. In order not to end up in stress-limbo, in a state of "freeze" without getting anything done at all, he started a routine of going through each day's to-do list and removing anything that was not actually due during that day. He could do these tasks after finishing that day's most important and pressing assignments, so why not put them aside until he was ready for them? And while he was at it, he looked for tasks he could delegate to someone else.

So, there he now was – working along in a comfortable tempo, feeling certain that he was doing the right thing that needed doing right now, and that nothing was forgotten or had fallen between the cracks. That gnawing anxiety was long gone.

TASK

Create your own morning routine. What do you need to do to get a perfect start to your workday? What would suit you best and how much time do you need to do it? Do you have to reserve time in the calendar to stay clear of meetings during this important time?

Make it extra clear to yourself that during the coming week you will perform a morning routine every day. Schedule a time in your calendar and set an alarm that reminds you if you feel it is necessary. Refine the routine as soon as you think of something that might improve it, or move the steps around if it should make the process easier and run more smoothly.

GAIN

If you begin every day by getting an overview of all the tasks, priorities, and appointments that lie ahead in a systematic and organized way, it will become much easier to do the right thing at the right time. You will not work overtime nearly as much as you may have done previously because you will have a clear view of your situation and what lies ahead.

REWARD

If you create your morning routine and manage to do it every morning for two weeks, then reward yourself thoroughly according to your preferences. This will therefore be a postponed reward, but it won't hurt you.

AUTOMATE DAY 26:

PRE-EMPTING THE TIME THIEVES

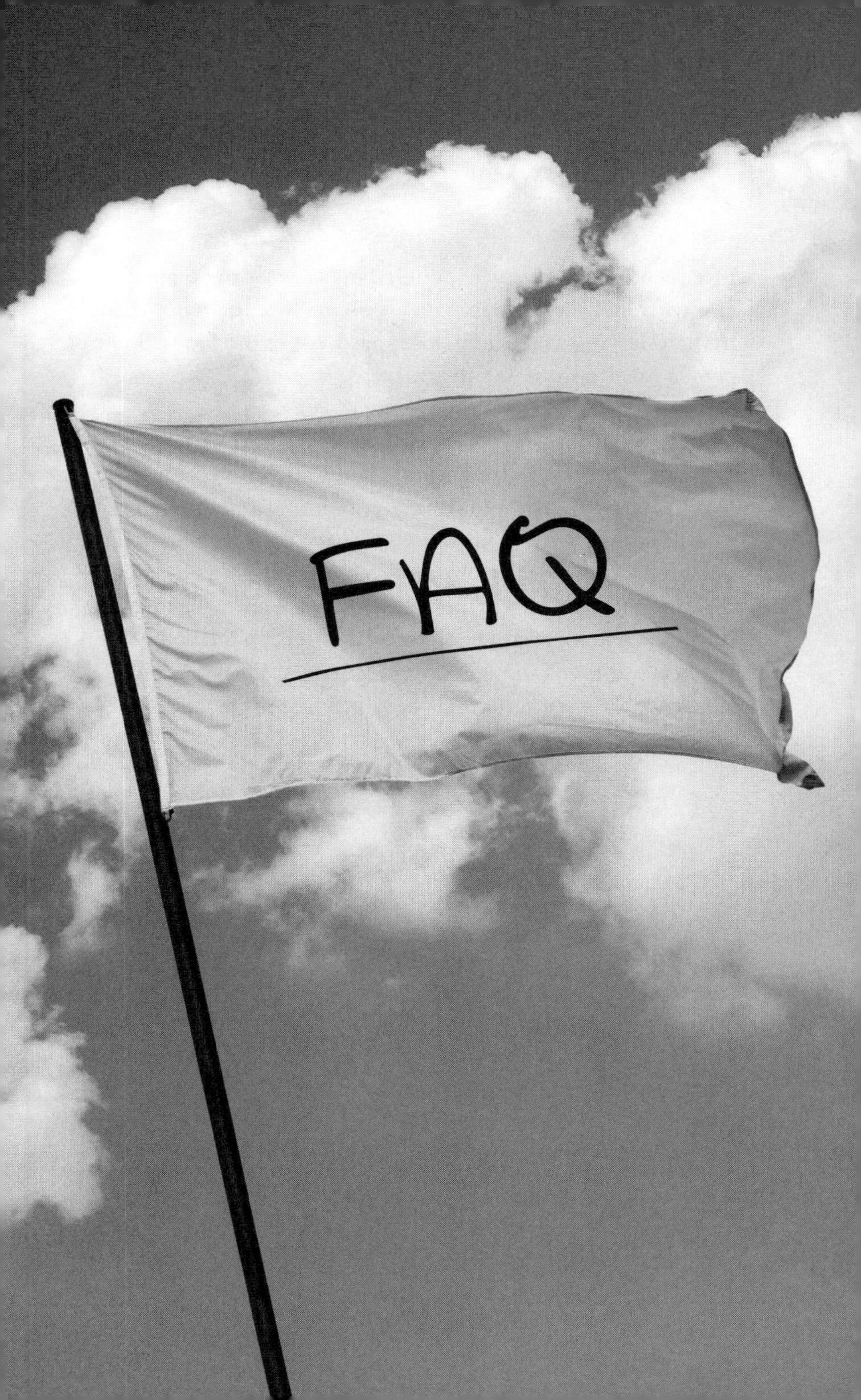
FAQ

{ ## Make it simple. }

I frequently ask the participants of my courses to do an exercise with me where we line up all events that interrupt them in their day and make them lose speed, time, and focus. Some people refer to these as time thieves.

In spite of all those years of team building and pleasant Friday coffee breaks, colleagues are often mentioned on these lists. As we are in the middle of a demanding and urgent task, a col-league pops into our office "to just ask something really quickly". We look up from our task and let go of our deep concentration to answer them, because we want to be helpful. Another time we might be the one who needs a quick answer. We lose our focus though, and in worst case it takes a while before we are back on track – just in time for the next knock on our door.

When the internet was still rather new, emailing lists on all kinds of subjects and topics was common and popular. But the administrators of these lists had a problem. Recently added subscribers tended to pose more or less the same questions as existing, older subscribers previously asked when they were new to the list. So there was a steady stream of similar questions, and this was when the concept of FAQ – Frequently Asked Questions – was conceived. The administrator would then send answers to the most frequently recurring questions to everyone, and thereby no longer had to reply to emails containing the same questions.

The answers to the questions you get interrupted about do not necessarily need to come from you personally. If you gradually assemble an FAQ document, then your colleagues can refer to it for their "quick questions" without depending on you being available to answer them personally. You will not be interrupted as often as before, and you will be much happier to see your colleagues when they now stop by.

TASK

1. Open up a fresh document (in whatever word processing tool you use). Write down a question you frequently get and the answer you usually give, e.g. "Question: ..." and on the row beneath, "Answer: ...". Make it simple. Don't mind the formatting too much, you can always go back to refine and adjust later. And it need not be a question you get often. It could also be about things that your colleagues need to do or certain tasks you have delegated to them. Perhaps it concerns "how you want things done" or your answers to a third party that your colleague can communicate with in your stead. If you really cannot think of a single question, then you have still made progress today. Eventually you will run into a question suitable for adding to your FAQ.

2. Save the FAQ document in a location that is easily accessible to the people it is intended for. If you share documents through a shared file server in your organization, then save it there. Perhaps you have a document management system and this is the obvious location to save it in. Or add it to your Dropbox account, to Box.com, or another of the cloud storage services. The important thing is just that you can reach it easily to update whenever you need to, without hassle.

3. Tell at least one colleague about your new FAQ and send them a link to the document, so that he or she can find answers to their queries quickly when you are not available.

4. Keep adding things to your FAQ as you come to think of them.

GAIN

Eventually, you will have created a bank of information and knowledge. Your colleagues – and perhaps your clients as well – will get answers to their questions much faster and you will get to work in peace to a greater extent. If you should feel uncertain regarding something or forget what you previously decided about something yourself, the FAQ will provide you with reminders and answers as well. If you still receive questions that you have already answered in the FAQ document, simply copy and paste the answer you already formulated into the response. It might not be a completely automated process, but close enough.

REWARD

If you create an FAQ document and present it to at least one more person, then reward yourself in the way you previously determined you could and would. Enjoy. You have taken yet another step toward creating an easier and smoother life.

AUTOMATE DAY 27:

FINE-TUNE YOUR NOTE-TAKING

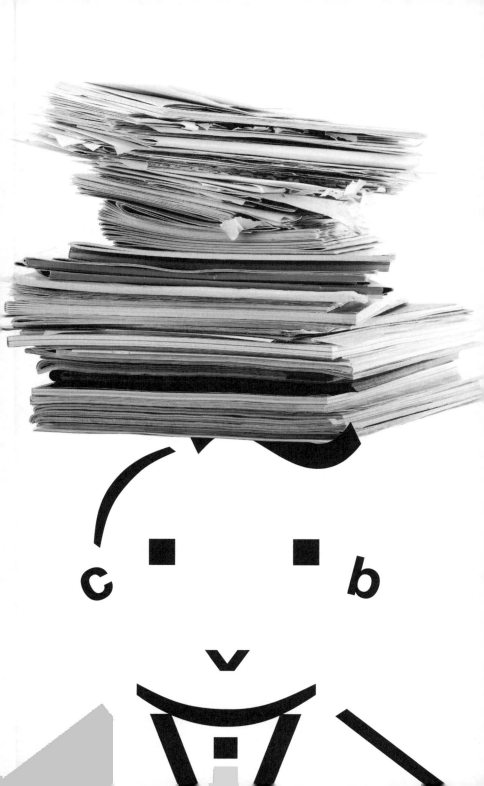

{ How do you ensure that the **to-do tasks** end up on your to-do list? }

Together with another one of my clients, a sales manager at one of the larger Swedish service companies, we had a long day ahead of us. He had been feeling that he was improvising too much lately. Most of the time he remembered by himself that he should have taken care of something, and had to finish it last minute. At other times he was reminded by a client who called and asked why he had not yet got back to them with something he promised to send a week before. And meetings – he certainly had a few every week. He usually had days with several meetings in a row, and one of his main challenges was therefore to find time for doing all the things agreed upon during these meetings.

We had set aside the entire day for scrutinizing and reworking the structure of his days at work. I began by asking him to write down absolutely everything he had to do into the tool he had chosen to keep his to-do list.

"All right. So far, so good," I said. "Now, are there any other tasks somewhere else?" "Yes, I might have some in my notepad as well," he replied. He pulled out a regular notepad and flipped through it. "These are my notes from different meetings. I usually use a new sheet for every meeting, and then make notes there."

"Good", I said. "And the things you agree on, what happens to them?" "Oh well, it often stays in the notepad." "OK, so in order to get an overview of all the things you promised you would act on and do something about, you have to flip backwards and forwards through all the notes and look for things that are practically to-do tasks?" "Yes, either through this notepad, or my other one." "Your other one?" "Yes, this one was so messy and cluttered that I got a new one a few weeks ago."

This is a very common trap. When a conscious process has not been developed to transfer commitments made during meetings to a place where other to-do tasks are stored, the risk of forgetting things increases significantly. But if you create a fully or at least semi-automatic process or routine that transfers any promises you made during a meeting onto your to-do list soon thereafter, it will become much easier to prioritize accurately.

TASK

Take a moment to think about how you make notes during meetings and refine your method. A few guiding questions would be:

1. What tool do you usually use?
   - a sheet of paper
   - a notepad
   - a document on your laptop
   - an iPad (or some other tablet)
   - something completely different.

2. When making notes, how do you distinguish between the things that you promise to do from all the other information? So that later, when you are skimming through your notes these actions are easy to find and you can identify the to-do tasks associated with them.

3. How do you ensure that the to-do tasks get transferred to your to-do list?
   - do you write them on the list by hand? If so, when?
   - do they end up on the list automatically because you sync your list somehow? If so, how do you ensure that they get the correct project tags, context, and due date whenever these are applicable? If you want to make this extra clear, grab a blank piece of paper and sketch out the process. Let your sketch begin with you sitting in the meeting and end with the tasks neatly in place, just as easily accessible and organized as any of your tasks. If you get ideas of how to improve the process and fill up the gaps (if there are any in the process), then create to-do tasks of what concrete steps you need to take to make the change.

GAIN

If you create an infallible routine that transfers everything you promise others on to your to-do list, you will make it possible to prioritize these among all your other tasks. You will do more of the things you promise clients, project participants, and co-workers than you used to. If instilling confidence and trust is important in your work, then you can imagine how important and valuable a reliable process like this is.

REWARD

If you have thought about how you take notes during meetings and what you then do with these notes by answering the questions above, you should definitely reward yourself in the way you have previously chosen to. If you also did at least something concrete about improving your working method, then reward yourself a little extra.

AUTOMATE DAY 28:

GO WITH THE INFLOW

{ Create an overview of where, how, and when information flows to you. }

We had taken a break during my lecture for a Swedish industry organization for consultants. They were serving coffee in the hotel lobby overlooking the beautiful archipelago of the Swedish west coast, and we were discussing to what extent good structure was or was not present in the participants' lives. Stefan, who spent much of his time travelling and who described himself as someone who tended to agree to more and more assignments and jobs, suddenly frowned and said: "But David, if you are only supposed to have one place where you gather and keep track of all the things you have to do, what do you do with the thing you promise a client over the phone while you are in the taxi to the airport?"

It is an important and wise reflection to make. These occasions tend to become pitfalls that make our well-thought-out structure falter. It is easy to focus excessively on the scenario of sitting by the computer in our office, comfortably by our desk with all our programs and materials readily available. But most of us have several other situations in our everyday lives when we receive information that needs to be converted into to-do tasks, saved as reference information, be defined as a new project, made note of as something we are waiting for from others, parked as something we want to do later but not now, and so on.

It all comes down to logistics, even if it is on a micro-scale. If we construct our flows of information consciously, we will need to put in less effort to make everything run smoothly.

TASK

Create an overview of where, how and when information flows to you, and how you take care of that information in a reliable and conscious way. Do this:

1. Download the flow-chart template from www.superstructured.com/inflows

2. Think about in what situations you are exposed to an inflow of information. These could for instance be:
   - during meetings
   - at your desk
   - in front of your laptop
   - when checking emails on your phone
   - via the phone while you are in a taxi
   - when you are at home and get an idea
   - when you are in the middle of a presentation before your team
   - during a lunch with a client
   - when you are flying and the "fasten seatbelt" sign is lit
   - when you are riding your bike
   - when you are driving
   - on the underground

3. For each and every situation, think about how you go about securing the information step by step in terms of things you need to do, things you are waiting for from others, information you will need at some point (but do not know when), ideas you want to park for now, or new projects to initiate. Refer to the template for examples of how you can create and clarify the process.

4. Look for gaps and glitches in the flows, where you do not feel confident of what to do with certain information, or places where you tend to make notes but then forget all about.

5. For every glitch you find, define a to-do task that has you doing something about the flaw or gap. It could be installing an app on your phone with which you can document what you agree on during meetings and from there send what you commit to doing directly to your to-do list. It could also be getting yourself a notebook for ideas that you always carry in your bag, so that you can make notes of and park an idea as soon as it occurs to you. It could also be making a habit out of emptying your bag or briefcase daily and process all the pa-pers you have put in it throughout the day to ensure that nothing gets left behind, is misplaced, or is forgotten. Or, you might need to do something completely different.

6. Once you are done, save the flow chart in a place where it is easily accessible as soon as you need it later on.

7. Also save the template so that you can redo the exercise whenever you notice that one of your inflow processes is not working properly. If you keep the template available and accessible, it will be easier to rebuild the faulty process and refine your inflow of information immediately.

GAIN

If you refine inflows of information and tasks, then you can rest assured that all the things you commit to doing will be duly noted and available on your to-do list. You will no longer strain to remember what you promised the client while you were on the phone, fewer things will be abandoned prematurely, and you will no longer have to receive those uncomfortable calls from people for whom you promised to do something and had forgotten all about.

REWARD

If you map out all the inflows of information you can think of and figure out at least one concrete thing you could do to refine your method further, then you definitely deserve the reward you have decided to give yourself when accomplishing changes in your structure.

AUTOMATE DAY 29:

REUSE AND RECYCLE

{   Get more work done with less effort.   }

Have you ever experienced "writer's block"? Have you struggled with phrasing and formulating an email in which you need to present one of your new products in such a clear and attractive way that the client simply cannot resist it?

We write and rewrite, formulate and erase, and phrase it again differently. Processes like these can take quite a bit of time, and if you are out of luck, you get stuck, and instead of progressing, you put the whole thing aside for now and start doing something completely different, even though you keep thinking "I should be writing that presentation" for the rest of the day as your guilty conscience grows.

But if you think about it, is it really the first time you have put whatever you are trying to compose in writing? Have you not written something similar before?

Few garments are as exquisite as a tailor-made suit. It fits you perfectly, it is fashioned from exclusive materials and it will last for years. But it takes time to create. If you let a bespoke tailor sew your suit, you will go through three stages of fittings during the course of several months. This means that there is only time to create a few exclusive suits, and they cost accordingly. Most of us do not require our clothes to be custom-made. We go to an ordinary store and buy ready-to-wear rather than made-to-measure. It might not fit perfectly and it's not be entirely unique, but it definitely suffices. As they are easier and cheaper to make, these types of clothes are sold in significantly greater quantities. The same principle applies to the texts you need to write. Either you can reinvent the wheel every time, or you can gain time and effort by reusing what you have previously written. You will finish more tasks and ultimately have more time for what truly matters.

TASK

Find a place where you will save all your brilliant texts, sentences, wordings, phrases, and formulations so that they become easier to reuse. It can be a common text document (such as a Word document), a document in a cloud-based app or even a dedicated notebook in a cloud-synced notetaking app whose name ends with "note". Do this:

1. Create a new document or notebook and name it something that feels obvious to you, such as "Useful phrases", or something else you like better.

2. Save it among your other digital reference information. But, beware. How easy is it to open this document with pre-written phrases and text? How many clicks away is it? The deeper into a folder structure you place it, the less likely it is that you will reach all the way down for it every time. If it feels too far away once you need it, it is. Think about how to make it easily accessible. Will you create a shortcut in a suitable location? Will you name it something that is even easier to search for and locate?

3. Find a formulation among all your sent emails that you might be able to reuse. Add this to your "Useful phrases" document for future reference and use it the next time you need to write or phrase something similar.

GAIN

If you save reusable text you do not have to stress and sweat every time you need to formulate something similar to what you have previously written. You will reply faster, deliver text with less effort, and be done with the tasks sooner so that you can move on to other things. You will get more work done with less effort.

REWARD

If you find a place to save your "Useful phrases" document and add your first text to the document, then you are well worth a reward.

AUTOMATE DAY 30:

PLAN AHEAD

{ In all its simplicity, the tickler file
is one of the structure tools that
I enjoy and work with the most. }

Quite a few years ago now, my desk used to be full of piles of
paper as well. One pile consisted of things I needed to read and
get up to speed with, but for which I did not have time for just
then. Another contained documents I was currently working
with, just not at the moment. And I stacked things I should
do in a third pile. At best, I had attached a sticky note to every
document which indicated what I needed to do with it ("Call
Peter"), but that was far from always.

You would think that it might be practical to keep everything
you need within arm's reach, but it definitely gave me more
grief than glee. I kept getting distracted from what I was currently doing by things I spotted at the top of the piles, and I
spent far more time than I ought to have rummaging through
the piles for things to do next. And to make matters worse, I
often found things halfway through my digging around that
I should have done ages ago, and which I now needed to do
straight away. And not to mention all the space the piles took
up. When working on complicated tasks, I need to spread out
all the material involved in completing it (such as documents,
correspondence, notes, sketches, and so on) on my desk, but
when the desk was cluttered with piles and other irrelevant
things, I got frustrated that there was not enough space for

the task I was working and needed to solely focus on. More than once I took refuge in a conference room where I could spread it all out on the empty tables without being distracted by anything else.

But then one day someone told me about a structure tool that was almost a hundred years old called a "tickler file". Do not ask me why it is called this, but it is said that the American lawyers who developed the tool also gave it its peculiar name. Anyhow, the tickler file is more or less a time machine for papers and other physical materials that, in a way, we can send to our future selves. The 44 folders of the tickler file, numbered by date, month, and year, made it possible for me to rid the desk of at least three quarters of the piles previously covering it. The remaining quarter consisted of things I could either dispose of or store away more permanently. But, it was not only a matter of hiding all that material from sight. The beauty of the tickler file is that we automatically get the specific physical material we need for today's particular tasks delivered to us. Hence we do not have to see what we do not need until the time comes when we need it.

In all its simplicity, the tickler file is one of the structure tools that I enjoy and work with the most. It is a wonderful feeling having had someone (in my case, myself) prepare and organize all the material I will need during the day, and for it to be ready when I get to the office in the morning. I might add, I have a tickler file at home as well.

When I am giving lectures or courses, there are often many participants who have never heard of the tickler file or similar tools, so I am happy to spread the word.

You do not need to be handling a lot of papers in your work to find this veritable time machine useful. Most people nowadays receive less physical mail, scan more documents, and make most notes in digital programs, but it is enough for you to have only a few physical documents (or things, for that matter) that you do not want to forget to bring when you are visiting a client for the tickler file to be useful to you as well.

This is how a tickler file works: The system consists of 44 hanging file folders; 31 folders are numbered 1-31 (which constitutes possible dates of a month), 12 are named January through to December, and one is tagged with "Next year". In the box or the filing cabinet where you keep your folders, you hang today's folder closest to you and then let the rest of the folders for this month follow behind it. You then put in the folder for next month and then the folders representing the days of this month that have already passed. After having set that up, you hang the folders for the remaining months of this year, followed by the "Next year" folder, and finally the folders indicating the months that have already passed this year. And you are done.

Every day you will take out today's folder, empty it into your physical inbox and place it behind yesterday's folder, so that it now represents the same date but in next month. If you have a document you know you will need on Tuesday three weeks from now (but no sooner), you place it in the folder representing the correct date. You are then free to let go of it and work on what you need to focus on now, rather than having to remember it. You can relax knowing that it will be available to you just at the right time.

Two similar variations I have encountered are the accordion folder (which does the job of sorting the material well, but does not hide it from view) and a binder with dividers where the tabs indicate dates (but this method requires you to hole-punch all your documents or put them in plastic pockets). Both alternatives require more effort and hassle than just dropping your material into the appropriate hanging file folder.

If it is digital material you need to bring, you will remind yourself of doing so by either adding a link to the scheduled appointment in your digital calendar or set a reminder for a to-do task that tells you to bring it. If you always keep all your digital material synced and constantly available online, you will not even have to think of a solution – then it will not only be available to you when you are at the office, but everywhere you go.

TASK

Create a tickler file for the material you do not need now, but which you know you will need at a certain point in time. If you are one of the lucky few who is in no need at all of such a tool, then use today to work on one of the previous tasks that you did not quite finish.

1. Decide where you will keep your tickler file. In a drawer or a filing cabinet? Will you use a trolley for hanging file folders or get an appropriate box for your desk?

2. Now you need to get yourself hanging file folders. If you are working in a larger organization and are the least bit cost conscious, have a look in the archives or storage spaces for old, abandoned folders. Hanging file folders are nowadays regarded as somewhat outdated, which means that there are often plenty of discarded ones in good condition lying around in storage rooms everywhere. If you cannot find any, simply order them from your office supplies provider. The folders usually come in batches of 25, so you will probably need two boxes.

3. Make labels. You will need 31 labels numbered from 1 to 31, 12 labels indicating the months of the year, and one label that says "Next year". If you make them yourself (either physically or digitally), one standardized measurement of clear tabs for hanging file folders you could probably use is 2 by ⅝ (5cm by 1.3cm).

4. Place the labels inside the clear tabs, and attach them to the hanging file folders. This might take you a little while, so put on the radio or some good music while you are at it!

5. Finally, place the folders in order and then your new system is up and running.

GAIN

If you set up a system that provides you effortlessly with the material you need, when you need it, then you will not have to spend all that time searching for notes, travel documents, sketches, spreadsheets with calculations, and other things you need to bring to today's meeting. Let us say you save five minutes every day that you otherwise would have spent looking for things by having a tickler file. That totals to a little over 20 hours in a year, almost two and a half extra workdays in which you can do more meaningful things than look for documents.

If you have a tickler file or a digital equivalent, you will not have to be distracted by material that is irrelevant to what you are currently working on. And when those piles with things you felt you needed to keep an eye on are gone, you suddenly have plenty of extra desk space where you can spread out the material belonging to the task you are currently working on.

REWARD

If you decide on where you will have your tickler file, and at least get folders, you deserve that reward you previously decided to give yourself. If you assemble your entire tickler tile, then you are worth a little something extra. Well done and well prioritized!

CONGRATULATIONS, YOU HAVE CROSSED THE FINISH LINE!

DAY 31

{ ## Notice everything
that has improved. }

By completing these 30 steps divided into three separate phases – organize, focus, automate – you have given yourself more structured and pleasant workdays. I suggest you flip through the book and marvel at your accomplishment of having got through all these steps.

Think back to the day you first opened this book. How was your situation and life then? What was it that made you want to become more structured? What was a typical day like and how did you feel? What does a typical day look and feel like now? Notice everything that has improved. Grab a pad of sticky notes and write down everything you can think of that has got better, one improvement on every note. Stick all the notes on the wall and enjoy this visualization of your progress. Every note and every improvement is a victory in itself, so you have to feel proud of yourself and happy with the changes you have managed to implement.

Perhaps you thought of some really smart solution throughout the process that you would like to share. If so, feel free to write to me at super@stiernholm.com and tell me. I look forward to hearing from you.

Maybe you have not been quite as successful as you hoped and intended, and have fallen back into your old habits? If that is the case, then choose one of the days in the programme and repeat its task until it feels natural for you to follow your new habit without having to think about it. Then choose another task to continue working on. They say it takes 21 days to establish a habit, but there is no real evidence supporting this claim. On the contrary, the time it takes to create and implement a new method or habit varies considerably. The British researcher Phillippa Lally presented a study in the October edition of *European Journal of Social Psychology* in 2010, which suggested that it can take anything from 18 to 254 days before a habit is fully established and perceived as the obvious choice of action. So, continue for as long as you need. You have your whole life ahead of you to keep making changes, and even if you will not become super-structured in an instant, every improvement you make will give you more flow, efficiency, and enjoyment in your work.

Well done!

THANK YOU!

Thank you for taking the time to read this book. I hope that the time you have spent working through it feels like time well spent, and that you have experienced how you can achieve significant results by making even the smallest changes and refinements to your structure.

DO YOU WANT TO LEARN MORE?

Many people who begin making these types of alterations to their structure and working methods find that they want to continue making changes to create an even better structure. If you want to learn more, search for "productivity" and "efficiency" in the online bookstores and read whatever appeals to you. There are also a number of blogs that explore the topic, and on *www.superstructured.com/blog-tips* I have listed the blogs I find most interesting and appealing at the moment.

I regularly share tips on structure on the Structure Blog (www.stiernholm.com/blog) and in my weekly newsletter Done! (www.stiernholm.com/en/tips). You can also find information about the lectures I give on my website.

If you want help from me personally, you will reach me by emailing info@stiernholm.com. I give talks, hold seminars, and help larger groups as well as individuals in need of improving their structure, so you are more than welcome to get in touch!

REFERENCES AND FURTHER READING

Allen, David. *Getting Things Done: The Art of Stress-Free Productivity* (London: Penguin, 2001).

Amabile, Teresa M. and Steven J. Kramer, *The Progress Principle: Using Small Wins to Ignite Joy, Engagement, and Creativity at Work* (Boston, MA: Harvard Business Press Books, 2011).

Apgar, Mahlon. "Alternative Workplace: Changing Where and How People Work", HBR OnPoint Enhanced Edition (2000), first published in *Harvard Business Review*, May–June 1998. Accessed 10 August 2016. https://hbr.org/1998/05/the-alternative-workplace-changing-where-and-how-people-work.

Bodin Danielsson, C. *The Office – An Explorative Study: Architectural Design's Impact on Health, Job Satisfaction and Well-Being* (Stockholm: Kungliga Tekniska Hogskolan [Royal Institute of Technology], 2010).

Lally, P., C.H.M. van Jaarsveld, H.W.W. Potts, and J. Wardle. "How Are Habits Formed: Modelling Habit Formation in the Real World". *European Journal of Social Psychology*, 40 (2010): 998–1009. doi:10.1002/ejsp.674.

Lester, Toby, *Da Vinci's Ghost: Genius, Obsession, and How Leonardo Created the World in His Own Image* (New York: Free Press, 2012).

Masicampo, E.J. and R.F. Baumeister. "Consider It Done! Plan Making Can Eliminate the Cogni-tive Effects of Unfulfilled Goals". *Journal of Personality and Social Psychology*. 101, no. 4 (2011): 667-683. doi:10.1037/a0024192.